INTUITION
AND
SYNCHRONICITY

INTUITION
AND
SYNCHRONICITY:

*A Journey
to Fulfillment*

by Hazel M. Denning, Ph.D.

**ASSOCIATION FOR
RESEARCH AND
ENLIGHTENMENT**

A.R.E. Press • Virginia Beach • Virginia

A.R.E. Press
215 67th Street
Virginia Beach, VA 23451-2061

Denning, Hazel, M., 1907-
  Intuition and synchronicity : a journey to fulfillment / by
Hazel M. Denning.
     p.   cm.
Includes bibliographical references and index.
  ISBN 0-87604-437-2
  1. Coincidence. 2. Intuition. I. Title
BF1175.D46   2001
131—dc21

                              2001001817

Cover design by Lightbourne

*This book is dedicated to Leslie Ann Stormon,
my beautiful granddaughter, whose life
is a daily demonstration of intuition and synchronicity.*

Contents

Acknowledgments

First, I would like to express a deep appreciation to the many clients and friends whose case histories have made this book possible. All of them readily agreed to share their stories in the hope that it would help someone else with the same problem.

A very special thanks to my lifetime friend, Shirley Dixon, who so generously gave her expertise to the time-consuming task of proofreading the manuscript. Her suggestions and advice were invaluable.

To Connie Brooks and Gail Harris, who alphabetized the index, I am truly grateful. They saved me many hours of time in the final preparation of the book.

I also want to acknowledge the many friends who encouraged me to write this book and kept prodding me to work on it. Their continued interest in my progress was a positive factor in motivating me to complete it.

INTRODUCTION

When my second book, *Life Without Guilt,* was accepted, I sighed with relief and thought I was finished with writing. However, my intuition began to intrude, and I kept getting the mental message that I must write another book. It was to be about intuition and synchronicity.

Since these two concepts have captured my attention for many years, I have taught many workshops and classes about them. In addition, I have conscientiously worked at applying them in my own life. I had mixed feelings about putting my concepts in print. I was excited about the idea of sharing them because I feel they are so basic to a full awareness of who and what we are. On the other hand, writing a book is a truly demanding task that I did not anticipate with very much enthusiasm. An inner voice told me I had no choice; I had to do it.

At the same time I was writing, I was also investigating other books on the subject, and before long I realized that books about intuition are literally bursting into print. Apparently there are enough people responsive to this attribute, which we all possess, that it is time, in the scheme of things, for it to be presented in printed form to the public. I wanted my contribution to be different. I decided to approach intuition through examining those characteristics that promote intuition and enrich individual experiences in life.

When I was at Claremont College attending a psychology class, not one other student accepted my definition of intuition. The idea that any kind of knowledge could come from something outside of the physical world was a totally ludicrous idea. The other students believed anything you knew had to come from something you heard or saw some time after the moment of your birth.

At that time, as far as I know, there was no current literature about intuition. We have come a long way in twenty-five years. Of course there were books in the metaphysical field that discussed man's extrasensory capacities, but they had a limited following of readers. Today, practically all bookstores have large sections devoted to metaphysical literature, and publishers are grinding them out by the hundreds.

Everyone has intuition; we could not live without it. It is just more highly developed in some people than in others. Most people are unaware of their intuitive abilities and therefore do not use them to their advantage.

It is the awareness of this capacity and the conscious development of its use that separate the floundering individuals from the people who become masters of their fate. People who are masters of their fate are aware of their destiny, using each experience to further their spiritual development. The incredible payoffs for people who use their intuition are the seemingly miraculous synchronicities that occur regularly.

It is this connection between intuition and synchronicity that I have found so fascinating and so powerful. Because intuition enhances life so dramatically, I want to share my understanding of how one can develop and then implement this personal attribute.

That is the purpose of this book: to give you ideas and concepts that can help you develop and use this incredible capacity.

1

≋

SYNCHRONICITY

Synchronicity and *Intuition* will be the primary terms used in this book, but the subject of the book is really you, the reader. It is my purpose to communicate with your higher consciousness and, I hope, introduce you to the magic power in those two words. They literally hold the key to resolving many of the enigmas in your life. Do things never seem to work out right for you? Is your health a problem? Are you unhappy in your job? What about your family and your friends? Are your relationships compatible? Do you feel unloved?

Two incidents come to mind that will illustrate synchronicity and serve as a springboard into the subject matter of this book. I hope they also will provide the insight necessary for a better understanding and application of this magnificent universal principle.

At the time the first incident occurred, I was attending a lecture series at the University of California in Los Angeles. It was an evening class, and I always sat in the last row so I could leave in a hurry. One day a friend called and asked me if I knew how she could reach Carol Brown. I barely knew Carol, but I told my friend I would keep it in mind since she impressed me with the urgency of finding Carol.

The next week when I attended the lecture, I started to sit in my usual last-row seat, but I couldn't because some unseen force seemed to stop me. I proceeded down the aisle and started to sit again, but was literally propelled forward. Once more, I started to sit, but my thoughts were rebelling. I said to myself, "I don't want to sit way down here." Three times, I tried to sit but was pushed forward. I finally settled over halfway down the auditorium on the left side. I sat down somewhat disgruntled. The lady in front of me turned around as I relaxed in my seat. It was Carol Brown. I gave her the message and thanked whomever or whatever had guided me to that seat.

In the second experience, I had a phone conversation with a friend in Redlands who said he wanted to see me to discuss a matter of importance to him. As we talked, we discovered that we both were attending the annual conference on research at the Religious Science Church in Los Angeles. We decided to meet there and that we would discuss it later to make specific arrangements

I then forgot about it, and apparently, so did he. I drove to the conference with five friends. When we arrived, the place was crowded with people and cars. I let my passengers out and told them to find seats while I parked the car. When I returned, one of them was waiting for me in the lobby to tell me the only seats left were over on the far side of the balcony. We went there, and when I sat down, the man directly in front of me was my friend from Redlands, We expressed our surprise at the coincidence and discussed our business.

These are two excellent examples of synchronicity working

for me. What is the modus operandi of such ex
we have conscious control over them? Are they
by spirit guides who are aware of our need or re
manipulate events to our benefit? Or are they the result of a
foreordained destiny? Does our mind put out a thought or request that creates an energy pattern that solicits an automatic
response from the universal mind bank (whatever that may be),
which then responds to the thoughts we generate?

I am completely convinced that we control, consciously or
unconsciously, everything that happens to us, but my attempt to
understand the hows and whys led to an incredibly complicated
and interrelated set of events.

About three years ago, I decided to test this theory with a
simple experiment. I noticed that certain patterns of events were
consistently manifesting in my life. One was a daily occurrence.
My usual breakfast is a shake made with fruit juice, a banana,
yogurt, and powdered protein. In spite of all my efforts to be
careful, I often spilled some of the protein on the sink as I
poured it from the can into the blender. For a considerable period of time, I said to myself, "I always spill a little." I asked
close friends, "Why do I always spill a little? It is crazy, but I
cannot seem to help it."

This was a daily event for approximately three years. Then
one day, I declared firmly and with the most positive mental
thought I could muster, "I will no longer spill this protein on
my sink." That declaration was made more than a year ago.
Only twice in all of that time has any of the powder landed on
the sink, and those two times the spilled protein was a mere few
grains.

I should add that, whenever I thought about it, I would continue to say to myself, "I will no longer spill protein on the
sink." Even though I believe in the power of the mind to control
events, I was a little surprised at the immediate and continued
success of my experiment.

Another statement I have made to myself and many friends

is, "I always get lost when I go someplace unfamiliar." I could write a book on the adventures and misadventures I have experienced because I was lost. Since I traveled a great deal in my car, it was a considerable embarrassment and annoyance. Many times before I started on a trip, my thoughtful husband would insist on getting out a map and going over my route.

One evening, I spent more than an hour in Los Angeles, in pouring rain, trying to find the house where I was attending a weekend seminar. I was so annoyed with myself that I declared I would never get lost again. It worked for about three years, but then one night, again in the rain, I encountered a roadblock caused by a flood and was forced to take a detour. I drove for miles trying to find my way home. That so unnerved me that I fell back into the old pattern. About that time, I had a very dear friend who often traveled with me, and she told me she had no sense of direction and usually got lost if she was going to a new place. In sharing our experiences, the old pattern was reinforced in my own mind until I reinforced the positive message to myself. I never did completely overcome this annoying problem, but by being more aware of where I was going and how I would get there, I did manage quite well to reduce the "lost episodes."

The third project regarded my telephone, which for most of my life, has been extremely busy. One day it struck me how often calls came in simultaneously. I began to pay attention to this and to complain about it. I would frequently say to anyone who would listen, "Every time my phone rings, a second call comes in almost immediately." It fulfilled my expectations. I would sit for hours, working at my desk undisturbed. Then the phone would ring, and almost immediately, there would be another call.

It was so consistent and frequent that I ordered call waiting on my phone service. Sometimes even more calls would come within a minute of each other. This phenomena was so intriguing to me that I played with it over a period of about three years. It was quite uncanny at times. I might sit at my desk for a whole morning without an interruption. Then the phone would ring. Before I had a chance to do more than identify the caller, I would get the signal of a second call and, within a few seconds, a third and even a fourth call.

One day about six months ago, I had this simultaneous event occur three times in one morning. I sat in my chair and declared vehemently, "Enough is enough. I do not want this any more."

I cannot honestly state that it stopped entirely, but I can truthfully report that the occurrences have diminished markedly. One is faced with the provocative question: "How does this happen?" How can a thought produce a physical event? If this is literally true, it is also a terrifying thought. What about all the children who have wished their parents dead, or people who harbor rage and destructive thoughts against others? Obviously, all of these angry thoughts do not produce physical events, or we would all live in chaos. But it is a question worth addressing, and I'll discuss it further later.

There are those who believe we all have angel guides who help us when we ask for help, and some also believe that they have help from the dark forces. I do believe in guardian angels, but I find it highly unlikely that they are at all interested in monitoring all of our thoughts and carrying out the directives in them.

I have given this phenomenon considerable thought and read a number of books on energy, mind control, and the power of thoughts. The more I contemplate this human experience, the more awesome it becomes. It appears as if some super intelligence has orchestrated a magnificent system in which purpose and absolute order prevail. The laws governing this system are dependable and irrevocable. Conformity to these laws seems to bring order and harmony into a life; infractions of the laws result in disharmony and all manner of problems for the individual.

If current science theory is correct—that everything is energy in different forms—mind must also be energy. It is an energy endowed with the capacity to think, reason, and manipulate all other energies. Apparently it has power over physical events and even over physical matter. Put in other terms, everything in the universe is energy; the mind manipulates and controls the manner in which energy expresses in physical form.

I will discuss the conscious and the unconscious mind later. For now, recognize that we both manipulate energy and create our experiences, our health, our relationships, even our attitudes. The magnificent thing about this is that, when understood, it literally gives us the power to be the masters of our own destiny.

It is through the conscious application of this principle that we can create synchronistic experiences in our daily lives. Why is it that some people can always find a parking place while others drive around and around looking for one? I recall, many years ago, having a heated discussion with my minister about this. He finally said, "Do you mean to tell me you think God is interested in helping you find a parking space just because you ask for one?" I tried to explain to him that I believed that a law operating in accordance with divine design provides the means by which our requests are met when we use our minds for a specific purpose. If some intelligence that we call God is responsible for those laws, then, in that sense, you could say God answers our request. Those answers can come only when we align our minds with the law. God does not play favorites, nor is He/She capricious. The Bible states that God, "sendeth rain on the just and on the unjust." (Matt. 5:45) The law is impartial but always fair, and we can depend on that.

To return for a moment to finding the parking space, I don't think anyone was moved to accommodate me. I was directed at a subconscious level to go at just the right time to be there when there was a vacant space. Many times I have responded to a very subtle urge to leave or to delay my departure. When I arrived at my destination, a car would be pulling out right where I wanted to park. I always silently express appreciation when this happens. I believe appreciation is also an energy that creates a repetition of this phenomenon.

Many people call these experiences coincidences, and in one sense, they are. The dictionary says a coincidence is "The chance occurrence of two things at such a time as to seem remarkable, fitting, etc." I simply disagree with the word "chance" because I believe these occurrences result from a conscious or unconscious mental directive. The law of cause and effect leaves no room for chance events.

An understanding and application of this remarkable principle is the most empowering tool we have as human beings. The principle operates all of the time in our daily lives. The manner in which we apply it determines the degree of failure or success that manifests in our experiences.

I will share one additional example that clearly indicates how precise this technique can be. A few years ago, I realized there were a number of things I really wanted. At the time, I could not afford to buy them. I made a list, and it was a full page on standard-size lined paper, so there were about twenty items, including such unusual things as a silver Christmas tree, an old-fashioned meat grinder, a wooden chopping bowl, and numerous specialized kitchen gadgets. Shortly after I completed the list, one of the large charity organizations in Riverside held its annual rummage sale. I went, and to my delight, found every item on my list. The amazing thing was that the wooden chopping bowl was the exact size as the one I had inherited from my grandmother and that had been broken by one of my children. Even the carved design was so similar I would not have known by looking at it that it was not Grandmother's. The grinder had all of the attachments and also duplicated the one I had, regretfully, given away. As for the silver Christmas tree, I wanted it to put in the children's room. The one I found was exactly the size I had in mind.

This experience demonstrated for me the value of creating what you desire with your mind and believing you can have it.

Believing it will work and expecting the results is a large part of the success, perhaps the most important part. Just remember a simple little formula called DBE (**d**esire, **b**elieve, and **e**xpect).

If you sincerely want to bring synchronicity into your life, however, you will need to start developing your intuition. It is a major key to creating synchronicity in your experiences.

2

INTUITION

Intuition is not synchronicity, even though the two are very closely related. It is my belief that you must develop intuition in order to have significant synchronicity in life. Intuition prompts you to act and think in certain ways that create the results which contribute to well-being, allowing synchronicity to manifest..

The dictionary defines intuition as "the perception of truths, facts, etc. without reasoning; the immediate knowing or learning of something without the conscious use of reasoning; instantaneous apprehension." The word comes from the Latin word *intueri*, to consider, to look on.

When I was in college, I took a course in intuition as part of the psychology department curriculum. Fortunately for me, I had an excellent professor who had an open mind. I never did know her personal philosophy, but she allowed me to take exception to the prevailing belief of that era about what intuition is. The famous French psychologist Piaget taught that intuition is the recall of something that has been experienced in this life and then forgotten. He stated that it might have been seen or heard as a very young infant and retained in the subconscious mind, but that it had to have been put into the mind in the first place (in the current life) to be expressed as intuition. The idea that it could originate from a source beyond the current physical life was unscientific.

In that entire class of psychology students, there was not one who agreed with my point of view, and some of them were outright derisive of my belief that true intuition is communication with a dimension beyond the physical world. Since the grade received in that class depended upon a single paper, I spent a considerable amount of time on my paper and received an "A," along with a highly complimentary comment.

That experience really stimulated my interest in the subject. I wanted to understand more about the dynamics of this ability since some people seem to have highly developed intuition, while others show no evidence of having any such skills at all.

In the early thirties, a very close friend and I became involved in the Oxford Movement. This group advocated complete dedication to improving all of our relationships and listening to our inner guidance. We were intrigued with the possible benefits, and we also worked at applying the principles in our daily experiences.

One of my very earliest manifestations that demonstrated how intuition works occurred when I drove to Los Angeles to visit a favorite aunt. I had written her that I was coming and, though she had not replied, it never occurred to me that she might not have received my message. At that time, there were no freeways, and the trip to Hollywood from Riverside took about two and one-half hours.

As I reached Los Angeles, I felt a strong urge to stop at a service station and call her, but I ignored it. I drove on a few blocks, and the compulsion grew so strong that I actually pulled into a service station where I saw a phone. I sat there a moment and then decided I was acting foolishly and should not spend the money on a call that I was sure was not necessary. I started the car and drove on. When I arrived at my aunt's house, she was not there. I called my uncle at his office, and he told me she was out of the city on a visit.

I was profoundly impressed by this experience because I realized how powerful my hunch to stop and call my aunt had been. Could this kind of guidance become a regular thing in my life? I began to try to expect it, and sometimes, it brought spectacular events. Most of the time, I did not get much help in everyday activities. However, the outstanding events were noteworthy.

I went on a trip to visit my birthplace in Illinois. In the train station in Chicago, I was browsing in the magazine section because I had a two-hour layover. Suddenly, I was "told" to check my ticket for the time of my departure. I looked at it, and it clearly stated that I had two hours, in spite of the time on the four or five clocks in the station. I put the ticket back in my purse and continued to read my magazine, but the voice in my head insisted I check again. I did, and again I assured myself there could be no mistake. The ticket clearly showed a two-hour layover between my connecting trains. Then it was like a voice literally shouting, "Listen to me. Check your time again."

I walked to the gate where my train was to leave and asked the conductor standing there what time the next train left for Elgin. "In ten minutes," he replied. Needless to say, I went into mild shock, for my luggage was in a locker on the other side of the station. I ran to get my luggage and boarded the train as it was pulling out of the station. Had I missed it, my entire itinerary would have been disrupted, for there was no other train out of Chicago to my destination until the next day. This episode deeply impressed me with the value of listening to my inner voice.

The baffling aspect of this phenomena was its unpredictability. It always seemed to be a spontaneous occurrence and always happened when it was something important. In the early years of experimenting with this energy, I could not make it work on a daily basis. As time went by, however, I realized it was operating in my life more and more consistently as I projected positive and definitive thoughts.

If I lost or misplaced something, I would simply say, "I want it. Find it for me." I soon realized it was important to believe it would be found. One example clearly exemplifies what I mean. I needed an article for a paper I had promised to write by a certain date. I was unable to find it after looking in a number of places. I asked that it be found and then forgot about it. I had also discovered it was very important to forget about the question at hand, to not keep thinking about it. About eight days later, I was going past one of the filing cabinets, and I reached down and pulled open the bottom drawer. The secretary asked me what I was looking for as I was thumbing through the folders in the file. In a surprised voice, I said, "I don't know." At that moment, my hand reached the very paper I had requested eight days previously.

Intuition manifests in many different ways. In the example just given, I responded to an urge to open that drawer. I did not have the faintest conscious idea why, yet it did not seem at the moment to be strange or unreasonable. I was aware of what I was doing, but it was not a conscious, purposeful act. The only way I have been able to describe the feeling is that it is as if my conscious mind is put on hold and something motivates or directs me through a series of events.

The most dramatic example of this that I have ever experienced occurred a number of years ago when I was attending a conference. I was standing in my room, talking with someone, when I suddenly broke off the conversation. I grabbed my briefcase, dashed out the door, ran across the hall and took the elevator down. I hurried to the lobby and started down the hall to the right. After a few feet, I turned around and crossed the lobby and started down the opposite hall, passed the first door, and entered the second door. The lady there was trying to get my projector open to show slides to the workshop she was leading in five minutes. She had called for help from the hotel staff, but they, too, were unable to open the projector.

I opened it, explained its features, and left. Then I returned to my room. As I put my briefcase down, I suddenly realized what had transpired. I stood a moment in shock, amazed at the guidance that had motivated me through the resolution of that emergency.

I stated earlier that synchronous experiences seem to come at times of danger of some kind or when I will be seriously inconvenienced if I am not warned of some impending problem.

There have been exceptions to this, but in each case there was a considerable emotional charge involved in the request for help. Two examples will illustrate this:

At the time of this first incident, I was president of the Riverside branch of the American Association of University Women (AAUW). There was a very important letter that I was supposed to read at the meeting coming up in the evening of this event. In the morning, as I was preparing my agenda, I had put the letter on my desk so it would be ready to be picked up when I left for the meeting.

After dinner, I hurried into my study and reached for the letter, but it was not there. Frantically, I moved the papers on my desk looking for it, but it was definitely not there. The thought of explaining to those AAUW members that I had misplaced the letter was an intolerable prospect. I stopped feeling panicked, stood in the middle of my office, and closed my eyes. I said, "All right! I need this. Where is it?".

Instantly the word "kabala" came into my mind, clear and sharp. This did not make sense, but I opened a file and lifted out a folder with that title. The last paper in it was my letter. Hastily I put it in my briefcase and said a heartfelt "Thank you." Then I heard, mentally of course, "We could do that for you all the time if you would just listen."

How did the letter get in that file? Well, it was not something I knew or remembered. That day, a friend had come in to see me and asked about the symbols of the kabala. I had studied that subject with a bishop of the Antioch Church, so I had a large file of material. After sharing it with my friend, I had returned the folder to the file and inadvertently picked up the letter with the kabala papers. Since I had no conscious knowledge of filing the letter with those papers, I believe I received information from an extrasensory source.

Another brief incident will illustrate an immediate response that is not a specific answer but more in the nature of a hunch. We had a guest and her baby visiting us. When they were ready to leave, she became agitated because she could not find the child's blanket. Four of us were dashing frantically about the house looking for that indispensable object. The mother explained that the child would not go to sleep without it.

I went into the bedroom where the child had napped but I could not find it. My voice said "Put that blanket away," referring to another blanket folded on my cedar chest. I argued, with some annoyance, "I'll do that later. Right now the baby blanket is more important." However, the thought fairly pounded in my mind," Put it away *now.*" I grabbed the blanket up, and under it was the baby blanket.

There are limitless areas within intuition that can be explored. Intuition is a multifaceted capacity of all human beings and, perhaps, of all life forms. The previous examples illustrate the more common manifestations of this phenomenon.

At this point, we should discuss reincarnation and karma because I believe intuitive and synchronistic experiences can best be understood only by considering these topics.

3

≋

REINCARNATION AND KARMA

Reincarnation and karma may very well be two of the most controversial and publicized subjects in the fields of philosophy, religion, and spirituality. Since all major, and many minor, cultures have espoused reincarnation and karma, there are countless written explanations and defenses of it through centuries of time.

I would like to make it very clear here that I never attempt to change people's belief systems if they are comfortable and satisfied with what they believe to be "truth." I heartily subscribe to the maxim, "and the truth shall make you free." (John 8:32) However, I am also very sure that no one knows all the truth. My own life has been dedicated to searching for the truth about everything. No matter how cherished a belief, when I have

15

found evidence of a higher truth, I relinquished the old belief. Therefore, this book and this chapter are a sharing of the results of my own research in the hope that it will expand the consciousness of others who are searching for truth. Many are ready to let go of dogma and theology that are not substantiated by historical facts. Let me assure you that you can be a Christian and believe in reincarnation. When the truth is known, there is no conflict.

Perhaps the controversy of most interest to western cultures occurred in the sixth century A.D. The controversy raged over a number of years, killed at least one pope, burned all the books dealing with reincarnation, expunged the Apocrypha from the Bible, and launched the Christian churches on the path to totally repudiating this doctrine. The facts are there for anyone to read who is ready to know the truth.

An excellent book on this subject is *Fragments of A Faith Forgotten* by G.R.S. Mead. It is a collection of the remnants of the Gnostic teachings salvaged after most of their books and writings were destroyed. The Gnostics had fought valiantly to keep reincarnation in the Christian faith. Two popes who refused to relinquish the belief were Agapetus I and Silverius, and Silverius may have been murdered as a result, through the efforts of the Empress Theodoras.

Few Christians are aware that in 553, the Emperor Justinian summoned the fifth Ecumenical Council of Constantinople for the primary purpose of removing the writings of Origen, an early church father who had lived almost 300 years before and had upheld the teaching of reincarnation. At the same conference, the Apocrypha was expunged from the Bible of that period. The Apocrypha contained fourteen books that had been part of the Roman Catholic Bible. They referred to reincarnation, and for that reason, they were declared not to be authentic. They were removed from the Bible. Today, however, some bookstores do carry modern Bibles that include the Apocrypha.

A quote from *The Hidden History of Reincarnation,* by Noel

Langley, indicates the significance of this event in Christian history:

> That two persons, even though an emperor and an empress, in the sixth century could so influence belief even to the twentieth century may seem incredible; yet if reincarnation seems a radical concept today, it is thanks to these two figures and their manipulation of historical records to suit their own ends

He is referring to Theodoras and Justinian.

In spite of their efforts, however, reincarnation has continued to attract adherents throughout history. Many great personalities and historical events have contributed to the preservation and promulgation of this philosophy—also called *palingenesis* and *metempsychosis*—through the ages.

Both Egypt and India each have been called the cradle of this belief system. As far back as religious history can be traced, both countries espoused reincarnation; the only exception was one of the many sects in India. In fact, all of the major religions of the world, including Judaism, once accepted this philosophy.

Rabbi Manassa ben Israel, Hebrew historian, wrote:

> The belief for the doctrine of the transmigration of souls is a firm and infallible dogma accepted by the whole assemblage of our church, so that there is none to be found who would dare to deny it . . . Indeed there are a great number of sages in Israel who hold firm to this doctrine so that they made it a dogma, a fundamental point in our religion.[1]

---

[1]*Reincarnation: The Cycle of Necessity,* Manly P. Hall. Philosophical Research Society, Los Angeles, Calif., 1993, p. 80.

Many consider Manly Hall to be one of the greatest philosophers of this century. He founded the Philosophical Research Society, Inc., in 1934, in Hollywood, California. His life was totally dedicated to research and writing. He delivered more than 7,000 lectures in the United States and abroad.

He sought to integrate science, religion, and philosophy. He wanted to help individuals develop a mature philosophy of life and recognize their true place in the unfolding universal pattern. To this end, he wrote and taught all of his life. The book cited here is one of the best available on the subject of reincarnation. He listed the following early Christians who espoused the multiple birth philosophy: St. Augustine, St. Jerome, Clement of Alexandria, Arnobius (an early Christian writer), St. Justin, and St. Gregory of Nyassa. He also stated that the mystical sects of Syria—the Therapeutae, Essenes, Nazarenes, Gebers, and Johanites—accepted rebirth as the normal plan of the universe. These philosophies are all in the Christian tradition. Other great peoples of the world also espoused this belief. Egypt affirmed reincarnation. Orpheus, Pythagoras, and Plato are said to have received it from the Egyptians and passed it on to the Greeks.

The Druids included reincarnation in the foundation of their religion. It is taught in the early Vedas and all of the sacred books of India. There are more sects or versions of it in India than in any other country.

Many African and Native American tribes incorporate it into their beliefs.[2] Among the Native Americans there are many different and interesting beliefs. For example, one tribe laid their dead by the roadside so that pregnant women passing that way would find a body for the fetus. Winnebagos believed that if you lived a good and upright life and died on the battlefield,

---

[2]*Reincarnation: A Study of Forgotten Truth,* Walker, E.D. university books, New Hyde Park, N.Y., 1965, p. 64.

you were assured of reincarnation.[3]

In spite of the ancient origin of this belief, recent centuries also have produced large numbers of outstanding leaders who accepted the rebirth theory. It is interesting to note that, in these times, it was never the masses who adhered to the theory; the intellectuals, the great minds of their time, taught it. Their thesis was that reincarnation gave people responsibility and power over their own lives. It presented God as the just origin of an orderly and dependable universe, with laws that were totally fair and impartial. It left people with freedom to create their own destiny by the manner in which they respond to universal laws.

One excellent book for those who wish to know more about these individuals is *Reincarnation In World Thought* by Joseph Head.[4] Among those Head cited was Paracelsus, 1493-1541, a Swiss physician.

Giordano Bruno, 1548-1600, was an Italian philosopher, a friend of Queen Elizabeth, and an outspoken exponent of reincarnation. Because he refused to recant some of his teachings, he was imprisoned and tortured for seven years and finally burned at the stake. In his last statement, he said, "Every act brings its appropriate reward or punishment in another life. In proportion as the soul has conducted itself in a body, it determines for itself its transition into another body."

Edmund Spencer, 1551-1599, was a famous English poet, well known for his *Faery Queen*. William Shakespeare, 1564-1616, frequently referred to reincarnation in his famous dramas. John Milton, 1608-1674, a British poet; Benedict Spinoza, 1632-1677, a Dutch philosopher; and Gottfried Wilhelm Leibnetz, 1646-1716, a German philosopher and mathematician, all wrote about reincarnation as accepted fact.

In the eighteenth century, there were five personalities who believed in reincarnation and who left so powerful an impact

---

[3]Hall, pp. 69-70.
[4]*Reincarnation in World Thought,* Joseph Head, S.L. Cranston. Julien Press, 1967, p. 238.

on society that they must be included in this list of famous people: Emanuel Swedenborg, 1680-1772; Francis Marie Aroust Voltaire, 1694-1778; Frederick the Great, 1712-1786; Immanuel Kant, 1724-1804; and Benjamin Franklin, 1706-1790.

One of Franklin's statements is my personal favorite quote:

> Thus finding myself to exist in the world, I believe I shall, in some shape or other; always exist; and with all the inconveniences human life is liable to, I shall not object to a new edition of mine, hoping, however, that the errata of the last may be corrected.[5]

In the nineteenth and twentieth centuries, we find a plethora of literary personalities including passages about reincarnation in their writings. Head and Cranston list no less than 131 such individuals. The list includes Napoleon Bonaparte (who claimed to have been Charlemagne), William Wordsworth, Walt Whitman, James Russell Lowell, Count Leo Tolstoy, Henrik Ibsen, Emily Dickinson, Mark Twain, Robert Browning, Richard Wagner, Edgar Allen Poe, Rudolf Steiner, David Lloyd George, Henry Ford, H. G. Wells, Jack London, Edgar Cayce, Kahlil Gibran, Edna Ferber, Eugene O'Neill, Pearl Buck, Maurice Maeterlinck, Rudyard Kipling, and Sir Winston Churchill.

A number of years ago I attended a two-day conference when the speakers were advertised as ten of the great minds of our time. Carl Rogers, one of the most prominent psychologists of our century, concluded his lecture by stating that he had finally come to embrace reincarnation as a universal truth because it was the only philosophy he had found which could explain all of the enigmas, inequities, and inconsistencies in life. He was greeted by a loud and vocal standing ovation. Then, to the delight of the audience, the famous anthropologist, Margaret

---

[5]Hall, pp. 104-105.

Mead, took the podium and, looking down at Dr. Rogers, said, "How interesting that Carl has just discovered this. Some of us have known it all the time."

Inventors, philosophers, and psychologists who believed in reincarnation are well represented in the twentieth century. Among them we find Thomas Edison, Luther Burbank, Mohandas Gandi, Bertrand Russell, Gustaf Stromberg, William James, J.B. Rhine, Ian Stevenson, Gina Cerminara, Ira Progoff, Raynor Johnson, Carl C. Jung, and Sir Julian Huxley.

The belief also is common among people in the theater and movies. Glen Ford, for example, believed from the time he was a child that he had been a famous horseman. As a boy, he insisted he smelled horses.[6]

General George Patton pretended to be a general from the time he was a small boy, strutting around with his play sword. He declared to his mother that he had been a great general and that he would be one again. It is well-known that, in WWII, he was often familiar with foreign terrain and even the streets in a town before he arrived there.[7]

Dr. Denys Kelsey, English psychiatrist, was convinced by his wife's experiences that reincarnation was a fact, but he was reluctant about regressing his patients for fear they would recall too much and be overwhelmed. However, his wife was so persistent that he experimented with regressions anyway and became one of the early past-life therapists. I had the pleasure of meeting him over the phone on two of my English trips and to share our findings. His wife, Joan Grant, authored a number of books detailing her recollection of her former lives. Her Egyptian life was so detailed that Egyptologists learned from them many new and verifiable facts about Egyptian life and times.[8]

---

[6]*Fate,* February 1969, p. 34.
[7]*Fate,* March 1967, pp. 32-42.
[8]*Other Worlds, Other Lives: Discover Your True Cosmic Origins,* Brad Steiger, Inner Light Publications, 1995, p. 66.

Dr. Lewis L. Dunnington, a retired Methodist minister, upon reading *There Is a River,* the biography of American psychic Edgar Cayce by Thomas Sugrue, wrote, "Here is the book I have long awaited . . . I knew that someday a book on reincarnation must come out detailing Cayce's message on reincarnation and answering our probing questions in that field. This is it."[9]

In the last two decades, dozens of books have been written with this subject as the central theme. Since past-life regression therapy has literally exploded in the field of psychotherapy, there are now hundreds of famous individuals who accept it as a personal philosophy. However, questions of whether there is any real proof of this belief abound, and some therapists have other explanations for the results of past-life therapy. Still, as for its efficiency as a therapeutic tool, there can be no doubt. *It works!* People recover from all types of illnesses, phobias, and other problems once they recall what seem to be experiences from previous existences. We may very well not have the full or accurate explanation of why it works, but for a long period of time, reincarnation has been an excellent hypothesis to explain life as we experience it.

In 1980, the Association for Past-Life Research and Therapy, now called the APRT, was organized. Today, it has a membership of almost 1,000 people in seventeen countries. Many members have written books about their astounding findings. It is worth noting that many of these members who are also therapists not only were highly skeptical, but were total disbelievers prior to their personal experience with regressing clients.

There are three areas that I believe support the idea of reincarnation. Perhaps the least evidential is the *déjà vu* experience, the feeling of having seen or experienced something before. Probably everyone has encountered this in either a mild or dramatic form at some time. It commonly manifests in two forms. You meet someone for the first time and you feel that you know

---

[9]A.R.E. *News,* March 1968, p. 4.

them. I call this a soul recognition. It can be either a happy experience or an unpleasant one. This, of course, accounts for the "love-at-first-sight" encounters. Another type of the *déjà vu* experience is when you find yourself in a place you have never been and you feel you have been there before. The term *déjà vu* is French and literally means "seen before."

A friend of mine was visiting England with her teenage daughter. When walking through the rooms of one of the old castles, suddenly the daughter became excited and began describing the details of rooms they had not seen. In one room, she was annoyed because she said they had changed the furniture and one of the large wall hangings. The guide corroborated her statement. The daughter insisted she had once lived in the castle as a female.

Volumes have been written on the *déjà vu* experiences, and reincarnation explains such encounters more adequately and logically than any other rationale.

The second area which lends credence to the multiple birth philosophy is the entire field of past-life regression therapy. Readily granting that not all so-called past-life recall is a valid account of a previous life experience, there is a preponderance of evidence for assuming the validity of a large percentage of recalls. The fact that hundreds of therapists using hypnosis as a tool have inadvertently elicited spontaneous patient recalls of previous lives, recalls that resolved the clients' problems, is overwhelming evidence for accepting it as a truth.

The third area, that I believe is the strongest evidence for the validity of reincarnation, is the overwhelming number of children who report experiences which they claim to remember from past lives. A recent book by Carol Bowman, *Children's Past Lives: How Past Life Memories Affect Your Child,* is perhaps the best publication on this subject to date. Bowman has a son and a daughter who both once suffered from phobias. The boy was afraid of loud noises, and the girl was terrified of fire. The son's phobia manifested one fourth of July when he panicked following a loud fireworks explosion. Regression took him to a life in the Civil War, when he was a soldier and was killed by a cannon blast. Once he recovered this memory, his fear was totally eliminated.

In the case of Bowman's daughter, the regression elicited the memory of a fire in which she was trapped behind a falling beam and burned to death. She no longer feared fire following this detailed recall. Bowman was so impressed with these dramatic experiences of her own children that she began hunting for other children who might have had similar experiences. She advertised in numerous magazines, requesting case histories of children who had manifested memories of past-life events. The response far exceeded her expectations and became the subject of her book. It is a book I recommend to every parent.

My own experience also is interesting. I have two sons, born several years apart. At less than three years of age, each said to me, in a very pensive mood, "Mother, I used to have a different body, didn't I".

A friend of mine has a daughter who informed her kindergarten teacher that she used to have another mother and father. These spontaneous remarks by children from ages two to around seven or eight cannot logically be explained by physiology or neurology. Such comments also are too common and too specific to be accidental.

It is clear, from history, the experiences of professional counselors, and even the remarks of children, that past lives and a belief in their reality are common experiences. It is also worth looking at what, exactly, people believe about reincarnation. For many people, it means that we have all lived in previous bodies in former times. But that is no more than the framework on which the philosophy is built. One can study for years and never encompass all of reincarnation's multitudinous nuances. It provides a magnificent design for all of life's experiences. All of the inequities, the unfairness of life as many experience it, the pain endured by "good" people, handicapped babies, and even natural disasters can be understood and explained by reincarnation.

It presents a universe operating under fixed and immutable laws that are impartial, dependable, and irrevocable. All major religions teach some version of such universal laws, regardless of whether they ascribe to reincarnation. In the Christian tradition, the Bible states, "Till heaven and earth pass, one jot or one title shall in no wise pass from the law, till all be fulfilled." (Matt. 5:18)

Reincarnation postulates a universe with a designer or creator so all-knowing and caring that every creature is guaranteed equal and fair treatment. Nothing is accidental; everything has a cause and an effect. Most importantly, every individual has a purpose in life.

To really understand the seemingly unfair problems and disasters some encounter in life, we must investigate the purpose of life. Why are we here in the first place? A study of all the great religious teachings provides the same answer: Earth life is a spiritual journey to perfect the soul or spirit inhabiting a physical form. In my thirty-eight years of working with clients in regression, this one premise was reinforced by all clients who explored this aspect of their problem. In investigating their past, they did not find some god punishing them for their so called sins. What they did discover quite clearly were their own mistakes, often repeated over several lifetimes, which they were working to correct.

As one client, who was suffering a great deal in this life, said after reliving four lives in which she had been abused, "If I had not been so angry and mean, they would not have treated me so cruelly. It was my own fault all the time."

One thing stands out with dramatic clarity: It is not important what we do or the experiences we have; they are all part of life's lessons. In the final scheme of things, the only thing that really counts is our attitudes about ourselves and our fellow beings. Rage, jealousy, resentment, guilt, and hate all contribute to the compounding of problems that eventually must be resolved through as many lifetimes as it takes. Those negative emotions will be changed to loving and caring for others.

Sometimes I am amazed at how long it has taken human beings to recognize and manifest love. The virtues and power of love have been recognized as far back as we have literature. As many writers have pointed out, it has been recognized as man's highest achievement for centuries, but few practice it in their daily lives. Yet, there is no personal or global problem that cannot be solved by the application of love and concern for the welfare of another human being.

There are thousands of books on this subject. I recommend M.F. Ashley Montagu's *The Direction of Human Development: A Scientific Confirmation of the Enduring Belief that Human Love Is Essential to all Social Growth.* Dr. Montagu is a psychologist and an educator. He has written one of the most profound chapters on love to be found anywhere.[10]

Reincarnation includes and describes the entire spectrum of human experiences. It encompasses all of the enigmas of life and explains reason and purpose in each individual's destiny pattern. Life is not capricious. It is purposeful and orderly according to universal spiritual laws.

Karma is a significant concept in the philosophy of reincarnation and, perhaps, the least understood. For many people karma is a word that connotes something unpleasant. Actually, it is the same thing as cause and effect in science. It has the same meaning as the Bible statement, "whatsoever a man soweth, that shall he also reap." (Gal. 6:7) It is the result of any and every action, physical or mental. It can be good or unpleasant, as the case may be. Karma is life in a constant struggle to balance itself by bringing the current personality into harmony with spiritual law.

While I believe reincarnation and karma are physical laws, I

---

[10]Chapter 9, p. 199.

do not believe they constitute the highest truth. There seems to be good evidence that, when an individual recognizes his/her divine nature, karmic law is transcended and the pattern of repeating mistakes until they are corrected is no longer required. In Christian parlance, sins are forgiven and one is in a state of grace.

To put it another way, the Universe or "God" is not punitive. The only purpose of pain is learning. When the reason is learned, there is no longer any need for the distress. And what is the lesson to be learned? We are spiritual beings. We already are an inseparable part of the divine Source. Therefore, recognizing our divine nature and living a life motivated by love and service to our fellow beings erases and liberates us from karmic negative patterns. All souls are seeking self-realization, and we move as actors in a divine drama on that quest.

Let us not be deceived by the perfectionists. No one can be perfect, and striving for perfection is sure to bring defeat because our energy is directed to benefit ourselves. It is totally egocentric. We learn from our mistakes when we are motivated by love and acceptance of others. When this motivation is coupled with a sincere desire to serve, we live in a state of harmony with the divine plan. When we truly love, the welfare of the other is always paramount. Someone has said, "Love God, and do as you please." That is the simplest formula I have found because, if you love someone, you cannot do anything that would harm him/her.

4

≋

BLIND SPOTS

"Fortunately the truth does not depend on your acceptance of it."   Unknown

All of us have blind spots in our evaluation of things, all
things, from judgments of others to opinions on economics, politics, education, religion, and philosophy. You name it,
and we all think we know the truth about it.

Very often, we may be entirely wrong, and we react based on
a false premise. This can have a destructive effect on our relationships, both personal and professional. Listening to almost
any heated argument is a fascinating study in futility. No one
can really win because, often, both are approaching the problem from ignorance of some of the facts.

We can learn from past mistakes, however, our own as well
as mass misconceptions. Let's look at a few major ones. People
once were absolutely certain the earth is flat and that the sun

circles the earth every twenty-four hours. What about all the people who were killed because the doctors believed blood-letting cured illnesses? When the telephone was first introduced, businessmen refused to put any money in it. They said we did not need it because we had "modern" telegraphy, and that was adequate for rapid communication. I remember my mother scoffing at talking movies and stating emphatically that they were a passing fad. In spite of all the archeological evidence, there are still people who categorically believe the earth was created in six days. The idea that man can fly provides an excellent example of nonbelief. The early pioneers of aviation took an outrageous amount of verbal abuse before their dreams were established as fact. A more recent example is space travel; those pioneers were *really* considered crazy. Sister Kenny was verbally crucified by the medical profession for her work with infantile paralysis victims before the efficacy of her method of treatment was recognized.

Most of you are old enough to recall the controversy over butter and oleomargarine. One year butter is not good for you, and margarine is better for your health. A decade later, the experts reverse their judgment, and in another few years, it is reversed again.

In the morals arena, things get really heated. Whole families are irreparably shattered when a son or daughter marries into a different economic stratum, religion, or race.

More than one family has disowned a daughter because she got pregnant "out of wedlock." My own son refused to recognize his first grandchild because his daughter was not married. After two years, he could no longer stand the estrangement. He asked me to bring both his daughter and granddaughter to visit him because he was ill at the time. It was a happy reunion.

As intelligent human beings, we are going to have opinions—and often, different opinions—about everything. That is the result of everyone's education and environment. By what criteria can we determine the accuracy of any of our opinions or beliefs? For the individual on a spiritual path, which implies functioning in harmony with universal principles, this is a serious concern. We are responsible for our every act. If our behavior is motivated by erroneous judgments, we are going to make decisions that are harmful to the welfare of others.

Intuition can be a valuable tool here. Until we have developed it with some measure of dependability, however, we are at the mercy of our prejudices and preconceived ideas.

I believe that, on one level of our minds, the truth about any situation involving our life behavior is known. In other words, if it were possible for us to be always "tuned in" with our intuition, we would always act in the best interest of not only ourselves, but all others involved.

Since this is not likely at this point in our development, what are some of the methods we can employ to test the validity of our beliefs, our judgments, and our behavior? The most effective yardstick I have discovered is simple. I ask, "Does this behavior or judgment hurt or injure another person?"

However, it is by no means a simple or foolproof formula. Many times, wise decisions can be temporarily hurtful to others. I have in mind here the parent who has to make decisions regarding a child, which at the time may make the child very unhappy or resentful. Wise decisions must often be made on anticipated long-range results. Using this formula, the method still stands. The decision is made for the long-range benefits of the individual. But is it humanly possible to know the long-range benefits of a decision made at any point in time? I am sure the parent who demands obedience from a son or daughter in making major life decisions, such as the choice of vocations, the selection of a mate, or the choice of a school honestly believes that is best for the child, In many cultures, family tradition is so deeply entrenched that children are literally subservient to the whim of the parent. I use the word "whim" advisedly because, often, major decisions such as marriages and vocations are arranged for the benefit of the parents.

Frankly, I believe those who think they know what is best for any other person have a blind spot, and that even applies to their children or any other relative.

This places us in an untenable position. Are we never to advise those near and dear to us, especially when we think we are sure we know what is best for them? Here, we can differentiate between advice and a directive. When someone seeks advice from another they consider wiser or better informed than they are, it is then appropriate to share your wisdom or even just your opinion. When there is a truly good relationship between parent and child, the child will ask and welcome advice from a parent when facing crises or difficult decisions.

Even in such events, I believe it is important to help the person make his/her own decision, following a discussion of the pros and cons of the issue. If the advisor makes the decision, the questioner is robbed of the right to be autonomous.

I remember well the time my son was seventeen, and we were having a very heated discussion about his decision to quit school three months before graduation and go into the navy. He said with considerable vehemence, "Mother, you have always taught me that I have to handle the consequences of my decisions, whatever they may be. I am ready to handle whatever happens if I go into the Navy." We knew it was going to be very difficult because he was a sensitive, artistic young man. We felt navy life would be intolerable for him. But he was determined, so we insisted he talk with two navy personnel we knew and with his school advisor.

Everyone he consulted advised against it, but he chose to go. He went with our blessing. His navy career lasted only two years, and he managed a psychosomatic illness that got him out on a medical discharge. But he also grew up a lot in that time and had the wonderful experience of going around the world twice and visiting many other countries. He completed high school while in the service. I have never since questioned the wisdom of his decision. It was something he *had* to do. *There is*

*no way we can know the destiny pattern of another person, re-
gardless of appearances.*

Blind spots in our thinking block the flow of our intuition.
As we develop intuition, we eliminate the blind spots. When
we find ourselves in conflict with others, it is important to examine our attitudes and beliefs for what may be such blind spots
in our thinking.

Even with the highest motives and the most conscientious
intent, we can be out in left field. One of my most traumatic
experiences will illustrate this. As a child growing up, I thought
I had the most wonderful mother anyone could have. She was
understanding, gentle, and kind; yet, she expected and somehow received respect and obedience from my sister and me. In
my twenties and thirties, she had the care of my grandmother.
Since she was divorced, she alone supported them both. She
often said to me, "Honey, if I ever get like your grandmother,
give me a good kick in the rear."

My grandmother, a talented artist, was, in every sense, a lady
who had many blind spots. She was the victim of "the proper
thing to do as a Christian lady." She lived to be 94, and mother
suffered a nervous breakdown before my grandmother died.

When my mother reached her seventies, she lived around the
corner from me, with my father-in-law, so my husband and I
could care for them both. It was an excellent arrangement since
both of them needed help. My mother became more and more
like her mother; she was opinionated, critical of almost everything. After my father-in-law died, she was afraid to stay alone,
had three locks on her doors, and would not open her windows.
When she came to my house, she would say in a disapproving
tone, "That's *not* the way I do it." I always replied, "I know,
Mother. You do it your way at your house, and I will do it my
way in my house. Then we will both be happy."

For a number of years I walked from her house to mine in a
state of frustration and, often, anger because I was so upset. I
would go to her house determined that, no matter what she did,

I would not let it upset me. Then I would return home furious because I had been unsuccessful in helping her to change her attitude. One day, as I was walking along simply furious with myself because I was so upset, a voice spoke to my mind as clearly as if someone was walking beside me. It said very clearly, "You should thank your mother for staying here long enough for you to overcome this."

I knew exactly what the statement meant. I had been able to stay out of the lives of all of my children. I never gave them or my friends advice unless they asked for it. My mother was a different matter, however. I had felt I really had to keep my promise to her not to let her get like my grandmother. The voice I heard changed my life. It was so powerful that I completely let go of the responsibility for her. I learned to let her be what she had to be. It was her destiny, her lessons to learn. The change in our relationship was dramatic and immediate.

I was amazed at how easy it was to live with her eccentricities when I did not feel I had to change her. She had always been deeply interested in my work and the paranormal field. She had no fear of death, so we often discussed what she called her "transition." On one occasion, when she was having a sick spell and was in bed, she asked me to help her pick out the dress and the matching jewelry she wanted to wear when she died. Another day she said, "Isn't it fun to be able to talk about my transition. I'll bet not many people can do that." How right she was, and how sad that is. One of my goals is to help people accept the demise of loved ones as a normal part of life and the fulfillment of their destiny pattern.

Because mother had been a truly good person, lovingly devoted to all of her family, unselfish always, I often pondered her last ten years, which were very painful, including the total loss of her sight. One can never be sure, but I always believed she carried considerable guilt over her resentment toward her own mother and punished herself by attracting experiences similar to those of her mother.

I am hoping at this point that you have been thinking about your own blind spots. Have you found any, and how can you identify them? You may think you do not have any because you believe that what you think about any subject is right, is the truth. But we all have them. The question is, how can we identify our own blind spots and increase our intuition activity?

I believe there are a few indications we can use to evaluate ourselves. One of the most obvious ones is finding ourselves frequently in conflict with others. This is a sure sign we need to examine our own stance on whatever the subject of conflict may be. Another warning signal may be the casual remarks of our friends or loved ones. I shall never forget one comment from my husband. He said, "Watch it dear. You are beginning to sound just like your mother," Those can be fighting words, and my first reaction was a feeling of resentment. However, I controlled my feelings and thanked him. From then on, I really worked at changing my attitude.

Our ability to change and respond by taking any criticism as a contribution to our own spiritual growth largely depends on the dedication or commitment we have as individuals to our spiritual advancement. If we can put aside our egos and think primarily of our spiritual goal, not only will our intuitive capacities dramatically increase but we also will make choices and changes that reduce our blind spots.

By our very nature as human beings, we are all going to be different, and it is our right to be. It would be horrible, and we would be like robots if we were all the same.

What are the differences among a blind spot, prejudice, and our individual perceptions of what is good or bad, right or wrong? The dictionary defines prejudice as an opinion formed without taking the time and care to judge fairly. We may be prejudiced against certain religious beliefs, against doctors, against cultures not our own, and against other persons or things.

While a blind spot and prejudice appear to be the same in

manifestation, I think of a blind spot as resulting from a deeply planted erroneous belief in something. I believe it often comes from experiences in a past life. I shall not elaborate on that at this point. For the purpose of this chapter, I am using blind spot and prejudice interchangeably.

A third criteria for testing our own blind spots is a major one. It encompasses many of the social problems of any age. It simply asks, "Does our belief denigrate, belittle, or harm other human beings?"

Using this criteria, it is obvious that history is replete with the horrible cruelty humans have inflicted upon their fellow beings. While rage, revenge, selfishness, and financial gain often played significant roles, the belief that specific views are right and the "other side" is wrong motivated and still motivates many of our social problems today.

From the past, we have as prime examples the Inquisition and the Civil War. Currently, we have a plethora of conflicting groups all acting out a belief that they are right and the "other side" is wrong. A few examples are the abortion issue, the belief that women are inferior to men, the deeply entrenched attitude that black people are not as smart as white people, the belief that Asians are devious, and the belief that all non-Christians will go to hell. The list is endless, and none of these beliefs has any sound basis for acceptance.

Only in retrospect can we see the kind of progress that indicates a universe with a spiritual purpose. As an example, the Civil War was a tragic experience for thousands of people who were fighting for what they believed to be right. However, some had to be wrong in their point of view. Slavery was a social evil, and in the grand scheme of things, it needed to be abolished.

I believe that, as we become more sensitive to the needs of those with whom we interact, our own intuitive capacities will be enhanced. We will live in harmony, not only with our own destinies, but also in our relationships with others.

Society can change only as individuals change, and each one of us is responsible for adding the energy of our loving concern to the people with whom we interact, as well as for the welfare of a suffering world.

How do you eliminate your blind spots? Perhaps I should say reduce them, since probably none of us can totally eliminate them. Examine your fixed ideas about *anything*. Explore all of the angles. Reading is a wonderful way to acquire knowledge about any subject. Perhaps you have a blind spot about the paranormal field. Many people do. When I lecture, I am amazed at the misconceptions people have about parapsychology and metaphysics.

Parapsychology is a study of anything man can do with his mind that cannot be explained by his five physical senses. It includes all of the new information being disseminated in the many fields dealing with mind energy. What could be more important than a study of how to use our minds to enhance our lives?

The word *metaphysics,* according to the dictionary, is a study of the real nature of the universe. It attempts to explain reality and knowledge. What could be a more meaningful objective and intellectual pursuit? Yet, many people, not understanding the word's meaning, react negatively and believe it is anti-Christian.

A friend once said to me, "Why do you have to go off on a tangent? I take it on faith." My reply to her was, "Good, if that is all you need. I want to know what I have faith *in,* and I have found it." I like to remind my skeptical friends that Jesus said, "Ask, and it shall be given you; seek, and ye shall find; knock, and it shall be opened unto you." (Matt. 7:7) I am a committed seeker, and it has paid rich dividends.

As you become more free of blind spots, you see life from a new perspective. In the first place, you do not make judgments about anything because you know that we all are on our own spiritual destiny paths. There is purpose in all experiences and a reason for whatever happens. If we really subscribe to this philosophy, we can accept the difficult events in our own lives, as well as in the lives of others, without rage or resentment. Most important, we realize we do not have the power to change another person's destiny.

I am directing these words especially to parents who believe they have to rescue their children. You are not responsible for your child's destiny. You are certainly responsible for the way you treat your child. You can make it easy or difficult for that child to live out the destiny path designed for him or her, but you cannot change it without causing serious damage to that child. I believe our responsibility as parents is to provide an environment in which children can grow and reach their own highest creative potential.

I remember well my two psychic friends who, many years ago, when my son was only about ten years old, said to me, "This child has a very difficult destiny, and if you do not accept it, you are going to be on a rack yourself for many years." They were so right. Having been warned, I could more easily love him and let him be what he had to be, including his prison terms and his involvement with drugs.

Another excellent example comes to mind. A father came to me in great distress and filled with guilt. He asked me to help him understand where he and his wife had gone wrong as parents. Their son was in all kinds of trouble, and they felt totally responsible. I asked him if he felt responsible for his own life. After some discussion of the implications of this, he said that of course he did. I asked him what he thought gave him the right to assume responsibility for his son. He saw the error of his thinking.

This attitude can be a blind spot for many parents. Accompanied by an overload of guilt, it blocks the intuitive capacities

Why is this attitude of acceptance and letting go of personal control so important? Unless you do this, you will be so occupied with trying to solve unsolvable problems that your intuition will be on hold and of no use to you. Once you let go of your blind spots, release your compulsion to control everything in your life, and accept what you cannot change, your intuitive capacities will be released, and you will find yourself directed by that wonderful inner knowledge that you have had all the time. Your intuition is God's voice speaking to you. Listen to it.

5

≋

PATIENCE

Impatience is the road to confusion. It is a wide road and well traveled. From the motorist who fumes and rages over waiting at a stop sign to the corporate executive who bellows at a subordinate who is slow to comply with an order, human beings discharge quantities of potentially constructive energy into destructive channels through impatient behavior.

Recently, I was standing in line at my bank, waiting to make a deposit. The line was quite long, and the woman in front of me was doing a slow burn that finally erupted into vocal expression directed at whomever might be close enough to hear. Her body was in almost constant motion, her head turning from side to side as if she expected to find a solution to her problem by looking for it in the air surrounding her. She said that something should be done about this intolerable situation.

I must admit I was amused by her frustration and the personal pain she was creating. Finally, I could restrain myself no longer, and I suggested in a friendly voice that I shared her frustration. I told her she was hurting herself by letting it get her so upset, and it would certainly not make the line go any faster. She admitted I was right, and for a few moments she was quiet; soon, however, her eyes once again began to dart about as if looking for a solution, and she began muttering under her breath.

I sometimes wonder if impatience is a cultural thing or innate in human nature. I have just about concluded that it is cultural, since there are societies that seem to be much more patient—with life, with their children, and with each other. Impatience seems to stem from western culture which, for centuries, has placed a premium on "getting ahead," being the best, having the most. Competition, rather than cooperation, has dominated western culture and others for millennia.

Millions of children never enjoy their childhood because they cannot wait to be old enough to have a car and to be independent. As young adults, they want to start at the top of the financial ladder. The exploitation of children to be the best in sports, in music, in the arts, and in education is a tragic but integral part of western culture. The cost in human suffering, physical injuries, and psychological damage is incalculable.

Certainly there is nothing wrong with having goals and working at being the best you can be, but that is the key: being the best *you* can be, not being better than someone else.

Most people are impatient with themselves a good deal of the time, feeling they are inadequate, clumsy, stupid, slow, untalented, ugly, and any number of other negative attributes. Perhaps the area in which we need to learn the most patience is with ourselves. Second in importance would most certainly be with our families. Few children are fortunate enough to have patient parents. From early potty training to scholastic achievements, we push and prod them to be better than they are. I am not underrating the importance of encouraging them to be good students, to live with honesty and integrity. Obviously, as parents, we are obligated to help them develop into responsible citizens.

To clarify my point, I will cite three case histories from my files. The first involved a mother and daughter. The girl was fourteen at the time and failing in school, even though she had always been a top student. Her mother came to me because, as she put it, she had reached the end of her rope with the girl. Every night, she made her daughter study, but she met with such resistance that every evening was an ugly battle. The girl would promise to do her studies in a few minutes and then procrastinate, and this would go on until almost ten o'clock, when the mother would clamp down and literally force the girl to sit down to study. She even sat beside her daughter to make certain that she complied.

I suggested she stop trying to make her daughter study. She protested vehemently and said that the girl would most certainly fail and lose her A standing. I explained that her daughter was actually behaving this way to declare her own autonomy, and when she succeeded in making her mother lose her temper, she felt in control.

The mother found this hard to accept, but finally promised to stop pushing her daughter to study. In our discussion of the problem, I told her I thought the girl had too much pride in her past achievements to actually let herself fail. I also suggested that a temporary failure might be preferred to a constant battle.

The mother finally agreed to say no more about studying. For a few nights, the girl made no effort to study. The mother was so upset, she flung herself onto her bed and broke into a tearful outburst. Hearing her, the girl went to her mother and asked why she was crying. The mother described how she had tried to be a perfect mother and how she believed she had failed her daughter, who she loved so much. The girl put her arms around her mother and said, "You could never be a perfect mother, but I love you just the same. Please trust me, and let me be responsible for myself." This was a true success story. Their relationship was vastly improved, and the girl ended the school year with her usual A record unbroken.

The second story involved a mother and her young son. She epitomized the patient mother. I knew her from the time her son was about four years old and watched her numerous times as she dealt with difficult situations. He was a very strong-willed child and, at times, a real challenge to her patience. His father was a busy executive and not home much of the time. He totally supported his wife's philosophy in raising their son, however. Physical punishment was never an option, but rules were to be obeyed, and the son was required and expected to conform.

I recall a specific situation one Sunday morning when the family was preparing for church. The child was four at the time. He began kicking up a fuss about something. The mother took him to the basement, where they could be alone, and entered into a lengthy conversation with him concerning his behavior. I could not hear her words, nor his replies, but she never raised her voice and they talked about a half hour. The rest of the family had gone on to church when they came back upstairs. He was no longer rebellious and, from all appearances, was a happy child again.

Because he was a strong-willed child, I wondered how she could be so patient with him. He grew into a wonderful and highly successful man. He had the kind of confidence in himself which served him well. Through the Depression, when many men could not find jobs, he was never unemployed and achieved high-level executive positions wherever he worked. Needless to say, he had the same kind and gentle patience with his three sons and one daughter. They are all well-adjusted and successful people.

A totally different kind of patience was practiced by another mother of two girls. I happened to be around this family fairly often and never once heard this mother raise her voice when she gently admonished them about something. The mother was an incredibly sloppy housekeeper, and this bothered her husband, since he had been raised in an immaculate, large, well-organized home. However, he, too, was a caring, well-adjusted person and exercised tremendous patience with her, as well as with the children. In the many times I was with this family, I never heard anything but concern for the person being addressed.

I will confess here my own response to this kind of laissez faire attitude. Many times, I thought there should have been stricter discipline and more control. It was only after many years had passed and those two girls had married and each had had four children of their own that I realized how balanced and responsible they were. Their children are now adults, and those children all have large families. They are all successful people and a tribute to their parents' and grandparents' loving treatment.

That family has been an inspiration to me. They taught me that patience and love expressed by parents create children who are more balanced and self-sufficient and who have better self-images than children who are constantly reminded of their shortcomings and faults.

I recall an interesting PTA meeting where I was one of a panel of speakers. I said that praise causes a child to want to please, whereas criticism only arouses resentment in the child. One father stated that he would praise his son if he ever found anything for which to praise him. I did not feel free to tell him he had done a terrific job of belittling his son if he could never find anything worthy of praise or a thank you.

For many years, I worked with young teens, both in the public schools and in a church as youth director. It was quite obvious to me that the children of military parents manifested the most behavior problems. Most of their fathers had little patience with normal adolescent behavior. I recall one large, tall, handsome boy of fourteen who gave his teachers continuous trouble. One day, he was sent to my office for discipline because he would not sit quietly in his classroom. When I said in a sympathetic voice, "I am so sorry. Are you in trouble again?" he burst into tears and responded in a choked voice, "Why am I always wrong, and the other person is always right? Why is my father always right, and I am always wrong?" His father was a captain in the air force.

It is true, of course, that different personalities are going to respond differently to the same stimuli. Patience and understanding with both children and adults pays high dividends in human relations.

Patience with "things" and patience with people are two quite different responses. Patience with people requires understanding and sympathy, or better still, empathy, the ability to feel the other person's feelings.

One of my own greatest lessons in patience came from an encounter with my eight-year-old son. He was an active, creative, impulsive child. One day he came home from school with mud all over his back. I was angry and started to give him a good scolding. Then suddenly, as if a wave of insight flooded me, I said, "Honey, I'll bet you had fun getting that way." His face brightened, and he replied, "I sure did, Mommy. I found a big mud puddle, and I sat down in it. It was such fun, Mommy."

I pointed out that his new suede jacket was a mess. His response was, "I'm sorry, Mommy. Take it out of my allowance, and send it to the cleaners. I'll go and shower now." As he started out the door, I stopped him and asked him to disrobe in the kitchen on the linoleum, where I could mop, since he was still dripping muddy water. The hall was carpeted, and he realized the wisdom of my request and complied cheerfully.

When I have told this story, I have been impressed with the different responses of mothers. A few think I was too easy and should have punished him. Most mothers believe I handled it the best way, but admit they would have had trouble being that accepting of his behavior. For me that experience did more to strengthen the bond between us than any other event. He felt that I understood. As the years went by and he was in really serious trouble as a teenager, that bond was never broken. When he was seventeen, he asked me why we didn't punish him the way his friends' parents did. I asked him if it would do any good; whether, since he knew he was doing wrong, punishing him would change anything? He said, "No mother. It would only make me hate you like my friends hate their parents."

Shortly before he was killed in a motorcycle accident, he said to me, with tears running down his face, "Mom, can you tell me why I do the things I do? I really hate myself for what I have done to you and dad, when you have been such good parents to me."

I explained to him that I understood he could not help living the destiny he came to fulfill. He knew what he did was wrong so he had to pay the penalty for that. I could not condone his behavior, but I did love him.

A very dear doctor friend who was psychic told me our son had been a monk in three lives and that he had come back this time to "live it up and learn how the other half lived." From the time my son was about four, he would not eat meat because he said animals had as much right to live as we did. This attitude could conceivably have been a carry-over from his monastic days.

I have always believed he contrived his death before he did any more bad things. It seemed a bit ironic that he gave his helmet to his best friend just before the accident, in which he was thrown thirty-four feet and landed on his head.

I have always been glad that I did not listen to family and friends who thought I should be harsh with him. He died with a strong bond of love and understanding between us.

The last thing I would want is for any reader to think I was a paragon of virtue in dealing with my son. For many years, I struggled with rage and actually broke the small blood vessels in my neck from anger so powerful I could not control it. I often talked with my son, smiling and showing no sign of rage, even when I felt that the top of my head was going to blow off. I do have a lot of willpower, and the one thing that made such control possible, not only with my son but also with other members of my family, was my love for them and a desire to do what I thought was best for them. Since about fifteen years ago, when I found out my tremendous rage came from a previous life, I have never once felt that rage again. It has been a wonderful relief.

In the final analysis, perhaps patience is the ability to feel the other person's feelings, needs, and, sometimes, pain and to respond to all that with loving concern for their welfare. Possibly another word for patience is acceptance. If we accept another person just as they are, we will be patient with them because we know they are acting out of some deep need or compulsion within themselves, In other words, they are acting out of a psychological need that is uniquely theirs.

Patience is essential in order for intuition to manifest. Two remarkable things happen when we are patient with someone. First, we are tuned into that person. That, in itself, is a form of intuition because we are able to intuit their feelings. Secondly, we reduce the tension and negative energy in our own auric field, which automatically plugs us into the harmonious field of spiritual or cosmic energy, the source of all intuition.

Now, let us examine patience with events, things, and situations. As I suggested earlier, one of the most common sources of impatience among drivers is traffic. Road rage has been the cause of a number of deaths. For a moment, let us substitute the word frustration for impatience. Waiting for clearance at a busy intersection, stuck behind a slow-moving vehicle on a two-lane road, or a driver cutting in front of you can elevate your blood pressure a number of points. As you sit waiting through a long series of stop signs, you can become almost apoplectic.

Being a perfectionist, organized, a don't-waste-time kind of person, it took me years to handle impatience with things and events. I often told myself that my primary lesson in this life was to learn patience. My profession as a counselor taught me patience with people, and that was not difficult for me, but the everyday events that went awry were a source of tremendous frustration. I recall once, when the vacuum cleaner was not performing right, I banged it up and down on the floor in sheer rage. My calm husband laughed and remarked, "It would make you feel better if you could put it across your knee and spank it, wouldn't it dear?"

His remark made me feel like an immature child and helped me to work on developing patience. Many years ago, I discovered that the minutes spent in waiting at a stop sign for a signal to change were a perfect time to relax, take a deep breath, and meditate on something positive. It worked like a charm and considerably reduced the stress. You can extend that formula to many other experiences in your life and almost eliminate stress caused by impatience.

I had a dramatic test of my patience when I moved into my current home almost five years ago. It was my dream house and had everything I had always wanted in a home, even extras such as a large skylight in the large, high-ceilinged living room; an atrium with a fountain in the middle of the house; two indoor, oversized planters; and a spacious floor plan.

From the moment I moved in, there were problems. When we arrived with the movers, the keys would not work, and we had to wait almost an hour for the landlord to bring the right keys. There was no handheld opener for the garage door, and I was reduced to using a padlock for three days. The keys were missing to the sliding glass doors. The hoses at the front and the side patio leaked at the faucet. One neon tube in the kitchen ceiling light was burned out. Two floodlights in the high ceiling of the living room were burned out. The connection leaked when I attached my washing machine. One bathroom had no towel racks, and the ceiling lights were burned out in the other bathroom. The coat closet had no rod to hang clothes and no shelf. The oven light did not work, and the knob on one of the surface burners was broken. It would take me almost a week to get the key to the mail box. When the movers were about to leave after emptying their load, I noticed I did not have a refrigerator. When I asked them about it, they insisted I had not told them to bring it. It cost me seventy-eight dollars for the extra trip back to my former residence to get that essential item.

Then came the pièce de résistance, though it was not the end of the problems. It was early Sunday evening, and I had been there three days and in and out of my kitchen door to the garage many times. I went out in my bathrobe for something in the garage and for the first time, when the door slammed shut behind me, it locked. Fortunately, I could open the garage door with the control from the inside. I went out and stood in my driveway and, looking to the sky, I said, "OK, God, now what do I do?" Without a moment's hesitation, my intuition clicked in, and I knew which house across the street was the right one for me to find help. I walked to that door, apologized for my attire, explained my dilemma, and asked if I could use their phone to call a locksmith. They were very sympathetic, insisted on serving me tea and freshly baked cookies. The man of the house called a friend who was a locksmith. He was there in a few minutes, and not only did he fix my door lock, but he promised me he would bring me a garage-door opener the next day. That couple turned out to be the best friends for me of all the people in my block.

I did one more thing, standing there in my bathrobe on my driveway. With immense satisfaction, I said, "God, no matter what happens to me, I am not going to get angry or be upset." I had a wonderful feeling of being in control. I felt as if I had graduated somehow in the school of life.

Words cannot describe the wonderful sense of peace and well-being you feel when you handle each event with patience and acceptance. Of course, the best part is that, when you are tuned into your intuitive capacities and being prompted by that intuition, synchronicity then becomes a commonplace in your life.

6

≋

ENTHUSIASM

E nthusiasm is perhaps one of the most powerful creators of energy. When you feel enthusiastic about something, your entire body responds with a surge of energy.

Of course, there are many levels of energy. There is the vigorous enthusiasm that is expressed in violent physical activity such as dancing, running, swimming, and many other body expressions; and then there is the quiet, inner enthusiasm that creates goose bumps.

Life is indeed dull without enthusiasm, and yet there are many people who never experience this wonderful emotion. They wake up in the morning dreading to face another day, and they go to bed at night exhausted and feeling defeated by life. You can be absolutely sure that your intuitive capacities are going to be just as enthusiastic or as dull as you feel.

I remember deciding when I was quite young that I would never be bored. I would find something interesting or valuable in every experience I encountered. I must confess it was not always easy, but it was worth the effort because it made life so much more interesting and exciting. Excitement may be another word for enthusiasm. When we are enthusiastic about something, we are excited about it.

Probably all of the inventions and important discoveries have been made by people who were enthusiastic about some idea that challenged them. Their enthusiasm was the very energy that activated their intuition. This, in turn, provided the insights or information that led to their successful development of that original idea.

One of the major features of this kind of enthusiasm is the complete confidence of the individual in the idea. No amount of ridicule or rejection can deter the efforts of that person to complete the goal.

Let's look at a few examples. One of the first that comes to mind is the Wright brothers. They were absolutely convinced that man could invent a machine that would take him into the skies. If any two people were ever ridiculed, they are certainly prime examples. Then came Lindberg. Fly across the ocean? To most people it was an insane idea, and most people probably expected him to fail.

What is the source of these wonderful ideas that come into the minds of human beings? We call them hunches or intuition but what are they really and where do they come from? Does an Infinite Mind contain all knowledge and parcel it out to humanity as we are ready to use it to further our evolvement?

I had a son-in-law who was an inventor. He invented the first miniature motorcars and boats that could be remotely controlled. He started the sport of racing these tiny cars on weekends in the Los Angeles area. I recall the weekend that he brought his little sailboat to Riverside, and we all stood in amazement as he maneuvered it on Lake Evans. He stood on the shore with the control in his hand, and that little boat responded instantly to the instrument he was holding. At that time, it was like a miracle.

He was eventually employed by Mattel, the toy company, as an engineer, and invented many of their successful toys. He was a true scientist and had no interest or belief in metaphysics or parapsychology, so these were subjects that were never discussed in my presence.

After many years of this silence, I finally dared to broach the subject by asking him where he got all the ideas for his inventions. I figured this was a safe question. He thought a moment and then replied, "I don't really know. It comes into my mind, and if I follow the idea exactly, it always works. If I change any part of it, it doesn't work. I can't explain it."

I had the courage at the moment to laugh and remark, "And you say you are not psychic." Everyone at the table laughed, and we dropped the subject. Many years later he actually saw the apparition of his sister-in-law, once while he was alone and a second time in the presence of his wife, who also saw it. The sister-in-law had died a short time before. It shook him profoundly, and he no longer rejected his wife's metaphysical concepts.

A client once asked me if he could improve his capacity as an engineer by developing his intuition. I told him I thought he could, and for a few sessions I worked with him in an altered state in which he requested that he be given help with an idea he had. He did not have a degree in engineering and felt handicapped because of this.

In three weeks, he presented his company with his invention. They complimented him on his idea. Since they could not use it in the manufacture of their product, they sold it to another company for $20,000.

I had another client who was employed by a munitions factory during the war. He told me that he would get clear, complete, and detailed visions of inventions to be used in the factory. On one occasion, he received details of an invention that circumvented an entire step in the manufacture of a strategic part for an airplane motor. When he demonstrated his invention, it was immediately accepted, and the machinery was adjusted to eliminate the unnecessary step in the process.

Neither of these men received any payment for their inventions since they were employees and whatever they produced was the property of the company. However, I was aware of their enthusiasm over what they had done. Both of them were consumed by excitement over the creative process that was unfolding in their minds and driven by enthusiasm as they pursued the process of bringing their idea into physical reality. Their reward was the exhilarating feeling of the successful creator. That energy seems to have the capacity to release the intuitive process in the individual.

Of all the experiences that will generate enthusiasm, perhaps the most powerful one is falling in love. I am talking now about that powerful emotion aroused when there is a soul recognition between two people. The excitement and enthusiasm one feels is unequaled by any other emotion, and enthusiasm is kicked into high gear as the two people become sensitive to each other's feelings and emotions. Often, the intuitive bond is so pronounced that the two people literally tune into each other's thoughts.

In people who are highly sensitive, this communication is recognized and mutually pleasurable. In less sensitive persons, the communication occurs at a less obvious level. It still occurs and frequently is responsible for the compatibility the couple enjoys. Should the relationship deteriorate, this intuitive bond usually is broken, and such communication no longer manifests between the two people.

No one can give you enthusiasm. You have to find it or generate it for yourself, and it will be different for each person. I had a friend some years ago who absolutely believed he had been the architect of one of the beautiful cathedrals in England. He came to me to be regressed so he could re-experience the thrill of creating something that beautiful and that important.

He was somewhat disappointed and considerably deflated to discover in trance that he had been one of the workmen on the building. He had been an artisan with special skills and had worked on the designs and trimmings of the outside. He was especially proud of the cornerstones he had lovingly wrought. But the thing that did impress him, as well as me, was that he had taken so much pride in his work and had been so enthusiastic about what he was doing that he literally felt he was an integral part of creating that cathedral.

He was more than just a master mason. It was that enthusiasm he had felt about his creation that had remained in his subconscious mind and, in this life, had manifested as the memory of creating a cathedral. In this life, he was a highly creative and gifted individual and very involved in metaphysical subjects and paranormal investigations. He was also very intuitive.

As you have been reading, I hope you have been thinking of something about which you can be enthusiastic.

The best time to generate enthusiasm is when you awaken in the morning. Do you greet the day with excitement in anticipation of what the day will bring, or do you groan and wish you could go back to sleep?

If you put some energy into it, you can become enthusiastic about almost anything. Even the trivial can become exciting. I recall an incident that will illustrate this. Years ago, I had a vegetable garden, and when I brought lettuce into the kitchen, I would be a basket case over the slugs in the lettuce. My thoughts exploded into phrases such as "Ugh, the slimy, repulsive, ugly things!" My flesh would crawl in disgust if my fingers came in contact with one.

Then one day, I became aware of my reaction and realized how ridiculous it was for a grown woman to be so affected by a tiny creature, especially since I thought I had reverence for all life. I even took spiders outside, when I found them in the house, to release them into the grass. I decided to explore one slug. I put it on a dish and became quite fascinated watching it stretch out and move slowly across the surface. The most interesting thing about it was the two tiny antennae that stretched out but rapidly retracted if I touched it. As I studied its movements, I became really excited about the pattern on its body. I got my magnifying glass and studied the beautiful design on its back.

It is difficult to describe the emotional response to this simple experience. I felt an overpowering sense of wonder and rapture over the magnificence of nature, which is so lavish in its expression in all fauna and flora. Needless to say, I have had real trouble killing slugs following that fantastic experience, and the feeling of revulsion is totally gone. Now, I take a moment to enjoy again the intricate design on the back whenever I encounter one.

While we are thinking about nature's lavish productions, let us take a moment to marvel at the mineral kingdom. Have you ever really given your full attention to the mystical shimmer of an opal or the radiant emanations of an amethyst geode? What about a diamond? I never cease to marvel at the scintillating beauty of a ring I have with two large stones. Whenever I wear it in my car, I hold it in the sun's rays and feel emotional excitement over its beauty. It never fails to generate enthusiasm in me over the incredible elegance of a tiny stone.

My son-in-law's favorite hobby was stone faceting. He had hundreds of gems cut from the rocks he had collected. Nothing pleased him more than to have the time to go rock hunting. To find and recognize the hidden beauty in an ordinary-looking rock engendered tremendous enthusiasm in him. As I have indicated earlier, he was highly intuitive.

While I never had the time to become involved in minerals, I have always been interested in them and spent a fair amount of time reading about them, being aesthetically thrilled by their beauty at rock exhibits and gem shows. I can never pass a jewelry counter without stopping to admire the display.

If nature is not your bag, let's turn to ideas and people. Biographies of many great and successful individuals reveal that, when they became enthusiastic about an idea, whether it was a new piece of machinery or a more effective way to deal with delinquency in ghettos, nothing could deter them from making their idea a reality.

Perhaps it is not an exaggeration to state that our progress as cultures and societies owes an everlasting debt to those who become excited over an idea and have the enthusiasm to pursue it to fruition. Every positive idea makes a contribution, whether it is an organization to improve the welfare of abused children or an electronic device to make air travel safer.

If you are the energetic, self-sufficient type, a do-it-yourself kind of person, there is no end to the possibilities for you to improve the world in the fields of government, education, economics, food supply, ecology, religion, and so on. Get really enthusiastic about your ideas, and you will set in motion the intuitive energy that will lead you to accomplishing your goal.

Even if you believe you do not have any talents, with a little effort, you can become enthusiastic about something just for the mere pleasure you get from enjoying it. What about music? The great poet Longfellow called music the universal language and said it was essential to a healthy life. Music can create a variety of moods. Pick the style of music that you enjoy, and let it carry you on a wave of high energy that motivates you to a sense of enthusiasm about whatever comes into your mind.

Perhaps the easiest, simplest form of excitement is vicariously experiencing the enthusiasm of those who have accomplished unusual feats. Examples easily can be found in newspapers and magazines. Most people respond emotionally to acts of heroism or feats of valor performed by people in all areas of life. It may be an invention to save lives, a new miracle formula for a heretofore incurable disease, a dramatic act of heroism, or the chronicle of an individual triumphing over incredible odds. You can mentally identify with any of these and feel an enthusiastic response.

The bottom line is to hang on to an enthusiastic response to life even in difficult times. You have probably heard the old saying, "When the going gets tough, the tough get going." I am totally convinced that, if you can maintain an enthusiastic attitude about life and your own destiny, success will follow faster than if you are depressed and discouraged.

Another experience in my son-in-law's life, which was significant in his destiny, illustrates this idea very well. Before he was hired by Mattel, he had a wife and baby and was living in a trailer. For six months, he was unable to find employment. He had applications out in forty different places. Both he and his wife really worked at "knowing" there was a right job out there for his special talents.

Then one day, a stranger came to his door and asked if he would consider coming to work for Mattel Creations, a new toy company just getting started. They had heard of his inventions and believed he was just the kind of person they were seeking as employees for this new venture. He worked for Mattel until he retired. Both he and his wife always believed he could not find employment because that special place for him first had to materialize, and he had to be desperate enough to take it. If he had been employed, he would have refused it because he would have felt degraded and embarrassed to have his family and friends know he was working for a toy company. As this company became world-famous, his attitude changed. He remained enthusiastic about his work throughout the many years he was there creating new toys.

There is no way to prove what I am about to say, but the evidence from my own experience with people seems to substantiate my belief.

Everyone has problems. Since the purpose of life seems to be spiritual development, we could not grow spiritually without obstacles to overcome. When things get really difficult, it is well to consider that we chose many of our experiences before we were born. I remember one client in trance saying her choices looked much easier from the spirit world. She had no idea it was going to be so difficult down here.

Believe me, maintaining an enthusiastic attitude about life in spite of the adversities and painful experiences, does make the painful experiences a little less painful. At the same time, it heightens intuition, which then sparks synchronicities. If you are observant, you will begin to notice these synchronicities, and the more you are aware of them, the more common they will become. The realization of your own power in creating synchronicities is sure to feed your enthusiasm. Can you appreciate how powerful this simple formula is? Enthusiasm generates intuition, and intuition results in synchronicities:

Enthusiasm→Intuition→Synchronicity

I suggest an excellent morning affirmation that I have used for many years and that really does help to keep me enthusiastic.:

This is the day which the Lord has made; We will rejoice and be glad in it. Psalms 118:24

7

≋

IMAGINATION

When clients achieve an altered state of consciousness and begin to have intuitive impressions, many say, "Oh, this must be my imagination." This is especially true when the images they pick up are bizarre or from another time or place.

I always encourage them to continue with whatever they are encountering. What is your imagination, anyway? It is most definitely from your own psyche. Whatever is coming into your conscious mind has some relevance and meaning for you. That does not mean it is the recall of a previous life, though it often is, but it does have significance for you.

Closely allied to imagination is fantasy. If you can fantasize, there is no limit to what you can create in your mind. In my town, there was a young boy who delivered papers to a beautiful large house on a hill, with two lions in front.

He never passed that house that he did not imagine himself living in it. He grew up and became a very well-known architect in his town. Eventually, he had enough money to buy that house. He redecorated it to his specifications, raised his family in it, and entertained his friends in it and in the beautiful gardens around it. It was a veritable showplace filled with elegant antiques and artifacts.

He truly manifested his fantasies, and he often talked with me about them and the intuition that guided him for so many years in finding just the objects he wanted to furnish his home.

Imagination is a broad highway to opening the channels to intuition. Then, of course, wonderful synchronistic events automatically follow. His life is a perfect example of how the mind, using imagination, actually orchestrates a total symphony from inception to completion

Many of the simple things we take for granted today were spawned in someone's imagination. I was driving with a friend the other day, and she stopped to buy gas. As she got into the car, I remarked about how convenient it was to have a gauge in the car that told you how much gas you had in the tank. She asked in mild surprise, "How else would you know if you needed gas?"

Then I explained to her that, not too many years ago, you put a stick down into the gas tank to measure how much gasoline you had left. Sometimes, of course, you ran out of gas because you forgot to check it.

Someone imagined that gauge on the dashboard of the car. Someone also imagined the self-starter, which was a tremendous improvement over painful cranking. Then came automatic transmissions and cruise control. Air conditioning was a major boon for driving comfort. Comparing today's cars with those of the 1950s or earlier gives many awesome examples of what can result from the imagination.

When a creative person's mind imagines a completed

project, it seems to set in motion the intuitive process that provides the formula for bringing the idea into physical manifestation.

In the early part of the century, an official of the U.S. Patent Office declared that we might as well close the patent office because everything of importance had been invented. We can assume he had very little imagination.

All one has to do is contemplate our modern world to realize how inventions and innovations in every area of our lives have dramatically changed how we live, think, and respond to life.

Every time I use my fax, I am amazed at its capacities. I sent my Japanese "daughter" a fax recently, and it was transmitted immediately to her in Tokyo.

I watched a documentary on television showing pictures taken on the moon and Mars. I am without words to express the emotional thrill I get just contemplating the miracles of modern science and the wonders of a universe we are only beginning to understand and appreciate.

Then my mind takes off, exploring the dynamics of it all. Do we indeed live in a world that is primarily energy? Do our minds use that energy to create everything we manifest, from our health to events in our lives to the physical world, with all of its multitudinous forms of expression?

If this is true, and I have come to believe it is, then cultivating our greatest asset in this universal scheme should bring us success and happiness. Our greatest asset is the creative power of our minds, and using our imagination opens the door to incredible vistas of creativity.

Years ago, when Carl Rogers inaugurated his nondirective client-centered therapy he believed that man was entering what he termed a "mind age." He said that our tremendous advances in technology had not solved our social problems and, as human beings, we must discover and understand ourselves and take responsibility for ourselves. He believed that all of our modern inventions and conveniences had not made us a healthy or happy people.[1]

He was optimistic when he said, "A quiet revolution is underway in almost every field. It holds promises of moving us forward to a more human, more person-centered world."[2] He cited an organization called Self-Determination, which promotes the idea of changing ourselves and society, from negative and self-denying to positive and self-actualizing.[3] "Then he said, "This development comes closer to being an expression of, and an organization for, the persons of tomorrow than anything else I know. It is a strong indication that the emerging individuals I have tried to describe do, in fact, exist and are becoming aware of like-minded others."[4]

Exercising your imagination is one of the most productive ways of opening the channels to intuition. Keep in mind that you do not have to have a degree or an extensive education. Universal mind energy is available to everyone because it is there; it just *is*. Anyone can tap into it at any time, in any place.

One of the great advances in our culture, as I observe it, is the recognition that children are naturally creative creatures. No longer do we have the attitude that children should be seen and not heard. I lived through a period when children were considered to be less than human. Their feelings were discounted as of no consequence, and they were considered to be little blank slates upon which their teachers and parents wrote their life patterns and created their futures. I once heard a young father arrogantly brag, "I am going to raise the perfect son." I might add that his son went on to live a very tragic and unhappy life.

One day, my son said to me, "Mother, I don't think adults have the proper respect for children." I asked him why he thought that. He said, "Well, I went to the mower shop to get

---

[1]*Carl Rogers on Personal Power,* Carl Rogers. Delacorte Press, New York, N.Y., 1977. See Chapter 12, "The Emerging Person," pp. 262-275.
[2]Ibid, p. 290.
[3]Ibid, p. 276.
[4]Ibid, p. 277.

dad's lawn mower, and there was someone ahead of me so I waited. Then some other people came in, and he waited on them. Then two more people came in, and he waited on *them*. When the store was empty, he looked at me and said, 'And now what do you want, kid?'

"I was so mad by then that I looked at him and said, 'I came in here for a lawn mower, but now I don't want anything.' I turned and walked out."

"I don't blame you," I responded sympathetically. "Do you think I respect your feelings?"

After a moment of contemplating this question, he looked at me and said, "Yes, mother, I do. I think you are the only one I know who does." What a sad commentary on our treatment of children!

Recently, there was an excellent article about Bill Bradley, author, basketball star, and former U.S. Senator. He talked about imagination. He said it allows us to escape the predictable; it enriches our experience and shapes our joys in countless ways. Then he said, "Above all, it enables us to see beyond the moment—to transcend our circumstances, however dire they may appear—and to reply to the common wisdom that says we cannot soar by saying, 'Just watch!.'"

There is another area where imagination is of very practical value. Most people suffer from being too hot or too cold or both at different seasons of the year. Did it ever occur to you to use your mind to control your physical state? You really can do this with a little imagination.

If you are too cold, close your eyes and imagine yourself lying on the sand at the beach, with the sun radiating a full blast of heat on your body, or imagine yourself in a sauna or a Jacuzzi. Feel the heat permeating your body.

If you are too hot, close your eyes and imagine drinking a glass of ice-cold lemonade or your favorite cold drink. You could imagine yourself playing in the snow. Feel the cold air on your cheeks, on your body. Walk into a cold storage unit and see and feel the frost forming on the frozen meat and on the cartons of food neatly stacked on the shelves.

You will be amazed at the results of these simple mental exercises. Of course, you must do them with diligence and a firm belief that you can succeed. It can work even if you are skeptical, but it is far more effective if you expect results.

You create your own environment all of the time, whether you are aware of it or not. Why not use that creative power you have to produce the conditions you want in any situation? That same formula works in many other areas of your life. Stress, which is an almost universal problem, causes many physical ailments. Many years ago, I discovered my own "magic" formula for reducing stress. At that time, I really thought I was going to disintegrate. I was so stressed that I stood in the middle of my study, my mind in a state of total confusion. It felt as if my mind was going to fly apart. I had never been so disoriented. I was carrying a full load of responsibility for directing the activities of a large international association and a local organization. I was responsible for the completion of a research project with twelve employees. I worked long hours, seven days a week, and never took vacations or play time. On top of all that full-time responsibility, I was in a Ph.D. program, working for a doctorate in clinical psychology. I stood by my desk, trying to decide what I should do. Should I drop the Ph.D. program? It was obvious I had to do something to relieve the pressure.

As I stood there, my mind whirling, a thought hit me like a bolt out of the blue: "You are stressed only if you *feel* stressed." It was so powerful that I acted on it at once. I selected the most pressing responsibility and discharged it. I simply let everything else wait its turn for my attention. I wrote many letters with an apology for their tardiness. It worked. I have not suffered from stress since, and that was a number of years ago. This does not mean I do not experience pressure. One cannot live actively in this modern world and not encounter frustrations and bothersome inconveniences. But you can live without the kind of stress that is destructive to your health and emotional well-being.

Stress is not only unhealthy, it makes it almost impossible for intuition to manifest in your life. Stress is destructive. It solves nothing and interferes with clear thinking.

The next time you find yourself stressed, stop and use your imagination to see yourself totally in charge of the situation. Calmly and rationally do whatever needs to be done just for that moment. Another way of handling it is saying to yourself, "I will take one step at a time."

I once had a wonderful professor who taught us to give our attention totally to whatever we were experiencing or doing and not to fragment our thinking by trying to solve two or three things at the same time. "If you are looking at a rose," he said, "let your full attention concentrate on its beauty, its scent, its color. Imagine yourself communicating with its essence."

This professor made it sound so practical that I decided to try it. I was working as a youth director at the Methodist church at the time, and the many duties there and at all of my other activities seemed like a good test of his theory. So when I was at the church, I gave my attention totally to the program there and the people with whom I was working. There was ample opportunity to use my imagination. Planning a program for young teenagers was a real challenge. When I was there, I never gave a thought to my family or what I would cook for dinner. Often, I left the church telling myself that, when I got home, I must call someone whom I could not reach in the daytime, but I almost always forgot to do so because, at home, I turned off all thoughts of the church. It was quite remarkable to me that this system worked so well.

There is tremendous power in your imagination. As you create an idea or an image with your imagination, you have only to hang onto it and believe in it and you can create whatever you imagined. It may be an emotion or feeling within yourself that you want to change. It could be an important invention such as a way to reduce the hazards of space travel. Whatever it is, if you are serious about it, I believe you can make it a physical reality.

All of the wonders in our world today once existed only in someone's imagination. What an exciting thought for each of us to ponder. All of us can contribute something to our world, even if it is no more than imagining a reduction in crime and a greater concern for our fellow beings. Why not start today using your imagination to create a healthier, happier world?

8

GRATITUDE

Gratitude generates tremendously powerful positive energy and contributes to the intuitive skills of the individual. How often do you take time to feel or express a surge of grateful emotion over something that has happened in your life?

If you could see the aura around your body, you would realize how important this emotional response is. When you feel a sudden rush of gratitude, your aura literally explodes around your body.

Investigators who have made a study of auras describe this energy field in considerable detail.[1] They say that when an indi-

---

[1] *Thought Forms,* Annie Wood Besant, C.W. Leadbeater. Quest Books, Wheaton, Ill., 1969.

vidual feels a strong emotional sense of gratitude, the auric energy of the body flares out in a beautiful halolike area around the body. It also takes specific forms in the atmosphere around the subject. People who are clairvoyant often see this colorful energy surrounding the physical form.

The aura includes different colors, and even the mood of the person is reflected in the energy field. Clairvoyants report that the color reflects the quality of the thought. The form is determined by the nature of the thought, and the clearness of the outline is determined by the explicitness of the thought.

For example, if one has a euphoric religious or spiritual burst of gratitude, the color produced will probably be blue. If the feeling is general gratitude, the form will likely be an undefined patch of blue. If the person is expressing gratitude for a specific thing, the color blue will take a well-defined form such as a flower or a geometric design. It should be remembered that these colors and thought forms are in constant motion.

The bibliography lists a number of books on this subject, and I recommend reading these books because they introduce the reader to a little-known capacity we all have. Few people realize the power of their thoughts, and a study of this phenomenon is an invaluable aid in understanding ourselves and our unlimited capacities.

Some of you may be thinking, How can I feel gratitude when nothing is going right in my life? If that is literally true and nothing seems to go right for you, then it is high time you are grateful that you have a mind that has the capacity to change what you do not like.

I have in mind right now someone who is living daily in that dark energy. Whenever I talk with him, I hear nothing but complaints about how life has dealt him continual problems. He could be grateful that he has a family who loves him and takes care of him in spite of his ill temper. He could be grateful that he is intelligent and has a remarkable talent which he is no longer using because he is engulfed in his own misery. He has become increasingly angry over what he considers life's unfair treatment of him, and he is now so consumed with rage and bitterness that he can no longer function as a productive individual. All of the efforts of his family and friends to help him let go of his anger and resentment are ignored. He cannot hear or recognize that his condition is the result of his attitude.

In the mind that nurtures gratitude, there is no room for rage, resentment, jealousy, guilt, hate, or any other destructive emotion. Such an individual lives in an atmosphere of constant positive expectations. This state of mind is like a spiritual invitation to the universe to deliver pleasant and positive experiences.

An attitude of gratitude literally tunes you in to the intuitional component of universal energy. Intuition is not something you create. It is a power, a universal force which cooperates with you when your energy is compatible with it. Feelings and expressions of gratitude are like an open door to intuition. With a little effort and practice, you can be aware of the many events happening around you all of the time that will inspire feelings of gratitude.

Some of the happiest people I know have lots of problems. The life of one friend I have known for many years has been quite difficult. She has been through two divorces, raised three children mostly by herself, and put herself through a university to earn a master's degree in psychology.

Her children were ostracized in their neighborhood because she is a highly gifted psychic, and people believed she was evil. Her mother and sister refused to speak to her over a period of years for the same reason.

She would come bouncing into my house, the epitome of joyful vibrant energy, and laughingly say, "We had a whee of a time at our house this morning." I never knew whether it was a catastrophic event or something really nice, since her voice and manner always implied the latter.

She sees the bright side of everything in her life and constantly expresses gratitude for what she considers her many blessings. For her, there is always a purpose in the problems she encounters, and so she is grateful for every new experience. Whether the experience is comfortable or difficult makes no difference.

I have known her for many years and seen the results of her wonderful courage and optimism. Her children are all grown and have enviably successful careers. She met and married a wonderful man who has given her the mature companionship and lifestyle she always dreamed of having. She is famous in her own field and travels extensively.

She heads my list of people who genuinely live in an atmosphere of gratitude. It is not a front with her. She genuinely feels and expresses the joy of living on a daily basis. Life is a comedy rather than a tragedy for her. She has the wonderful faculty of seeing the humor in the daily vicissitudes of life.

Be retrospective for a moment. If you are thirty or older, you probably can look back on events you thought were tragic or unfair, yet in the long view, you now can see how they were a good and positive experience in our destiny path. If you could embrace the philosophy that everything is occurring for your best good all of the time, even though you cannot comprehend it, you could much more easily be grateful for each experience as it occurs.

Examine your options for a moment. What in your life inspires gratitude? What about some of the modern conveniences we all enjoy? When I was a child, I had to walk out into the freezing cold weather to go to the toilet, which was about fifty feet from the house. I remember dreading that cold experience so much I would wait as long as I could and then have trouble getting there before I had an accident. What did we use for toilet paper? The pages from a Sears or Montgomery Ward catalog. When I hear people talk about the good old days, I am tremendously grateful for bathrooms and flush toilets.

I am also grateful for refrigerators. I can recall all too well the days of the ice box. I have suffered many a backache after doing the family wash on a scrub board. I never cease to be grateful for my washer and dryer. Certainly I would include the garbage disposal, and yes, the electric mixer, blender, toaster, and can opener. My husband often gave me electric gadgets for birthday gifts, and he finally asserted that he had me all electrified. The mangle iron was a really special gift, for I no longer had to stand to do all of the family ironing. I felt a sense of gratitude every time I sat down to it. Now I am grateful for nylon and polyester. I have used my iron only about five times in the last five years, and then it was for table linens. I never pack for a trip without feeling a strong sense of gratitude for the clothing, even the fancy evening wear that goes into the suitcase and comes out at my destination without a wrinkle. Long ago I gave away my travel iron.

Take a moment right now to mentally inventory the everyday gadgets or things you use and take as a matter of course, giving no thought to how recently they were not even in existence. As they flow through your mental screen, feel a warm glow of thankfulness and then be aware of how good it makes you feel to express gratitude.

The environment we live in offers many reasons to be grateful. Nature is extravagantly lavish in creating beauty all around us. From a spectacular display of the northern lights or the rainbow to an everyday sunset through billowing cloud formations, nature provides indescribable beauty.

When I went to the Catskills in upper New York one fall, I was euphoric as I scanned the hills ablaze in every shade of red, orange and yellow. I had never seen anything as spectacular in fall colors. In the spring, nothing quite rivals the huge rhododendrons in Golden Gate Park in San Francisco. Then my thoughts jump to the Descanso Camelia Gardens near Pasadena, California, and I experience a joyous response just recalling those elegant white blossoms.

I can still experience the overwhelming awe I felt as I stood on the ramp below the Iguacu Falls in Brazil and welcomed the heavy mist that surrounded my body. It was like becoming a part of that magnificent, thundering waterfall.

The experience that most affected me emotionally was my trip to Sedona, Arizona. It was truly a spiritual experience. I went there to visit a friend, and I was totally unprepared for the unrivaled magnificence of the landscape. I was driving along, and as I turned a corner in the road, there before me was an immense fantasy world in multiple shades of red. Disney fantasies paled in comparison. It was like entering a totally new world. I had never seen anything like it, and for a few moments I was in a state of sheer ecstasy. I felt like I had been transported into a totally new and different world, Time seemed to stand still. I wondered later how I managed to drive, for it seemed as though I was not in the real world for a brief period of time.

Beauty can, and does, lift our emotional energy. If we recognize the opportunity it provides us to respond with gratitude, our entire energy field is recharged and enhanced. This increases our sensitivity to all stimuli and opens our intuitive channels.

Architecture is one more area in the physical world I will address. Beautiful buildings all over the world are available for everyone to enjoy. Who can look at our Capitol in Washington, D.C., and not feel a sense of pride. Think about the Lincoln Monument. What a thrill it is to approach the statue of Lincoln, especially at night when it is lighted. It feels as if one is standing in the presence of greatness.

When my friend and I visited Turkey, we used every word in our vocabulary to describe the beauty we saw in various buildings and museums. When we entered the Blue Mosque, we were so overwhelmed we just stood and looked at each other and said through choked voices, "No words can describe this." It was difficult for us to speak for a few moments. It is indeed a rare experience to be treasured when beauty touches our souls so deeply. It is well if we can recognize these special gifts life gives us and consciously express gratitude for them. This conscious act is registered in our subconscious mind with an added emphasis when put there consciously, and thus it enhances our intuitive capacities to a greater extent.

I would like to suggest that if you cannot travel to any of these wonderful places, picture postcards are a wonderful substitute. I have two postcard albums filled with beautiful scenes of animals and buildings. It is a real aesthetic treat to sit down, relax, and browse through them when I want to experience sheer beauty.

There is still one area of gratitude I have not addressed, and it is perhaps the most important one of all. Each of us can be grateful for our life and all of our attributes, whatever they may be. Many people are painfully aware of their shortcomings, their mistakes, their so-called sins. When I have asked clients to make a list of their positive and negative qualities, they frequently have a problem finding anything positive to report.

The truth is that mistakes don't count, but our motives do. Do you try to be a good person? Do you deliberately do things to hurt someone? Do you steal or lie? Are you dependable? Do you keep your promises? If you have a responsibility, do you discharge it to the best of your ability? Do you hold grudges? Do you gossip and enjoy spreading a bit of scandal? Are you sensitive to the feelings of others and give encouragement and support to someone in pain? Do you think you are ugly? Is there some part of your body you dislike? Do you feel inferior to other people?

Take a piece of paper and make lists of your positive and negative qualities. If you are honest, you will undoubtedly discover that the positive list is longer than the negative list. The most important thing is for you to feel gratitude for the positive aspects of yourself.

One of my favorite cartoons is of a little boy leaning over a table with his head in his hands, looking a little glum. He says, "I must be worth somethin', 'cause God don't make no junk."

When you can recognize that you are an actual expression of God, with all of your faults, you will be grateful for your spiritual heritage and stop playing the victim role.

If your list is heavy with negative stuff, then call a halt right now and declare your God-given capacity to change what you do not like. Rev up your gratitude barometer, shift your energy into high gear, and follow your hunches.

9

≋

ACCEPTANCE AND UNDERSTANDING OF OTHERS

Accepting other people as they are is one of the most diffi-cult attitude challenges we all have to face. Almost every-one is judgmental with friends, children, spouses, co-workers, parents, public personalities, and elected officials. In other words, we are judgmental with everyone we know or know about.

As intelligent human beings, we *do* have opinions about any-thing and everything. The big question is, do you think your opinions are better than those of others? More significant, do you believe your opinion is the only right one?

The all-time perfect example of a true bigot, in my opinion, is Archie Bunker on the television show *All in the Family.* I have been fascinated by that show for years. Archie is not a bad person, and actually he is very sensitive and caring about those he loves. He truly suffers when his values are violated. I am reminded of the episode when he was trying to get his grandson baptized against the wishes of the baby's father. Archie firmly believed that the very soul of that grandson was threatened if he wasn't baptized, and Archie was willing to go to any lengths to save the baby's soul. He suffered deeply at the thought of the child being denied this important ceremony. When he finally resorted to baptizing the baby himself in the chancel of the church and humbly begged God to accept his clumsy ritual, it was a genuinely touching scene. I can imagine that many watchers of that television episode were moved, if not to tears, at least to constricted throats.

Another poignant episode dealt with Michael's friend from Canada. He was a draft dodger because he did not believe in war. When Archie discovered he had a draft dodger eating Christmas dinner at his table, he was so upset he could not eat. When Archie's co-worker shook hands with the young man and accepted him, even though his own son had died in the war, it was too much for Archie, and he walked off by himself and sadly said he had to think it over. His deep pain was well depicted, and the viewer realized how totally Archie was committed to what he believed was right.

Time after time in that series, I saw a man who was totally incapable of seeing any point of view other than his own. I also saw the outrageous results of this attitude.

What does this have to do with intuition? Quite obviously, intuition cannot manifest in us if we believe we are always right, for then we never listen or give credence to any opinion other than our own.

A psychological evaluation of such a person would uncover numerous personality problems. Probably foremost would be a deep-seated fear of being wrong. Throughout my years of counseling, I have had numerous such clients, and they responded very well to regression therapy, which usually uncovered an experience in childhood or a past life during which they were traumatized for making some kind of a mistake and became fixated on the need to always be right.

There are other psychological factors present in these cases, but this is not the place for further analysis except to point out that there is hope for those who believe their opinions and judgments are always right. As I have suggested, regression therapy will frequently help people to be more tolerant of the opinions of others. When an individual ego is so fragile that it cannot tolerate exploring its own attitudes, there is little hope of changing that person. Unfortunately, there are many people in all cultures who do not have the ego strength to face their own blind spots, and therein lies the cause of the vast bulk of relationship problems.

Of course, we all have the right to have convictions and opinions on any and every subject. We would not be thinking human beings were that not so. The problems arise when we try to impose our ideas on others who have different perceptions. In the proximity of a family or a job situation, where individuals are daily thrown into close contact with one another, it can be difficult to be totally accepting of the opinions of others if they conflict with our own.

Whenever I am faced with any kind of relationship problem, I look for a solution or explanation in the basic principles of life. I stated in the beginning that we should accept other people just as they are. I believe we have no right to try to change another person unless they ask us for our help. The reason for this is a basic karmic principle: Everyone is on a spiritual quest that is uniquely and entirely that person's destiny. We each chose our path and the lessons we have to learn. As difficult as this idea is for many people to accept, my own lifetime experience of counseling people with problems has provided me with ample evidence that everyone has an immortal soul. This wise aspect of ourselves directs our lives at an unconscious level in accordance with and in response to our attitudes and behavior.

It creates experiences that will teach us the spiritual lessons we must all eventually learn.

If this truly *is* a principle, then it is obvious that each of us is experiencing exactly what we require to fulfill our destiny. We may analyze, but we do not have the right to criticize or try to change other people. They are exactly where they need to be at that moment in time.

It is interesting to note that, in some Eastern countries, people will not assist a farmer if his load has fallen into the ditch. They believe that would be interfering with his karma. He has created the problem, and he must solve it himself.

This may be carrying that principle of noninterference a bit far, because loving and caring for others certainly requires that we be compassionate and assist each other appropriately. Unfortunately, it is true that too many parents are enablers and actually cripple their children rather than helping them. Parents *do not* always know what is best for their child. Every child is another soul here on a unique spiritual journey. My formula for a good parent is one who creates an environment in which the child can be free to reach that child's highest creative potential.

I can recall many cases in which my clients were crippled because of loving parents who overprotected them. One is a vivid recollection because her parents were very dear friends of mine.

This little five-year-old daughter was the pride and joy of her parents. Her father was a perfectionist and expected perfection from his child. He never punished her physically, but his orders were delivered with such firmness that she rarely disobeyed. She was always dressed in the most feminine little dresses, and if they became soiled or rumpled, she was immediately changed. She was never allowed to play in the dirt, and her environment was kept spotless and germ-free.

She began sitting in the middle of the floor, holding her doll and rocking back and forth, declaring vehemently that the doll was her baby. Her parents explained that it was just a doll, but she would become very upset and insist it was her baby. Her mother finally asked me if I would help the child. I went to the home to "play" with her. I realized she wanted to be a baby herself so she could be free of the stresses her parents had put on her. Her play behavior clearly indicated she needed to be free of so much restriction.

I started her out with finger painting, which gave her permission to be messy, and she was. She took globs of paint in her hands, leaned down, and rubbed her face in it saying, "I am loving this." One day, she pretended she was a dog walking on all fours and hiked her leg up at the corner of the table, carefully eyeing me to see if I would disapprove. Whatever she did, I accepted as if it were normal behavior.

Her parents were both professional people and had hired a live-in housekeeper and baby sitter. This woman's reaction to my visits amused me. One day she said to the mother, "Do you have any idea what this woman does with your child? She allows her to do the most outrageous things." Her behavior was an excellent example of judging another individual without knowing all the facts.

I saw the child only about five times before her bizarre behavior stopped. However, in the meantime, I was able to convince the mother that the little girl must have more freedom to be an individual with fewer restrictions.

This mother and father wanted the best for their daughter, and both of them really worked at following my advice. A short time later, the mother called me to report an incident that she thought would please me and indicated that my advice had proven successful.

She said it had been raining, and the water had made a little river by the curbing. She found her daughter squatting on the curb and using a small stick to pretend she had a boat. The mother raced out to remove the child from this dirty puddle, but recalling my advice, she was able to restrain herself. She approached her daughter and asked as cheerfully as she could,

"Are you having fun, dear?" The child looked up happily and responded, laughing, "Oh yes, mother, this is so much fun."

My friend told me that, at that moment, she felt as if she had succeeded in being a successful mother. The problem was resolved, and this little girl grew up to be well-adjusted and highly successful in the business world.

Another case I often recall was the sixteen-year-old girl who came for help because she felt so inadequate with girls her own age. She described her parents as so loving and caring that they protected her from all the normal experiences every child should have.

She could not have a bicycle because she might get hurt. She could not ride a horse for the same reason. She was not allowed to spend a night away from home and, so, missed all the slumber parties her school friends talked about. She was driven to and from school and any activity in which she participated. She had no boyfriends because she was considered too young for that. Her summary of her own situation was that her parents had so crippled her normal development that she felt like a little girl and was totally incapable of relating normally with her peers.

The sad part of these kinds of stories is that parents who really love their children have no realization of the rights of their child to live life fully, using the difficulties they encounter as children to develop their capacities to cope with life. As parents, we should give them comfort and support in handling their problems. We should not shield them from the normal, but often painful, experiences that the child's own destiny has determined.

I hope I have been successful in convincing my readers that we have no right to make judgments or attempt to control another person's life, including our own children. We do not own them. As parents, we are to nurture, encourage, and, by example, teach them integrity and the importance of love and concern for others.

There was a family in our church that included three daughters. Everyone loved and respected them, and in all the years I worked with them, I never heard a negative or unkind remark from any of them. One day, I asked the mother for the secret of their success, and her reply was simple. After a moment of reflection, she said, "Well, I suppose it is just that we always try to be considerate of each other." How simple, yet how profound.

All of these remarks about accepting a child's unique life pattern in no way implies that discipline is unimportant. A child who lives with overly permissive parents will be unable to develop self-discipline and will encounter many difficult problems as an adult.

No two children should be treated alike. This is where developing intuition is so important. If we are intuitive about each child, we will deal with the problems of each one according to individual personality needs.

In our family, for example, we had two boys. One was adopted; the other was a foster child the same age as our adopted son. The foster child was dependable, absolutely honest, obedient, and introverted in his relationships. Parenting him was a pleasure. But this also created difficulties for us as parents because there was no reason ever to punish him, and our adopted son was constantly in trouble. Fortunately, the boys developed a strong bond, which was good.

When the foster son came to us, he stuttered. In our loving, accepting atmosphere, his stuttering totally stopped in two weeks, never to return.

If I had ever punished the foster son physically, I knew the relationship between us would never be the same. On the other hand, our adopted son needed to be punished because it relieved his guilt for a brief time. I realized this one day when I let him out of a punishment I had promised if he broke the piano keys again. Half an hour later, he brought me the ruler I used on his legs when punishment was in order and said defiantly, "Here, punish me. What are you trying to do, spoil me?

My husband and I both believed physical punishment was a last resort, and we seldom used it. However, my intuition indicated that our son needed this type of discipline in order to relieve the guilt he felt at times, and this incident convinced me of its importance in his case. Years later, when he was a grown man, three regression sessions uncovered the past life in which he had been a slave runner. He had come into this life with a heavy burden of guilt, and he lived an extremely painful and difficult life and died of cancer at age 54.

His regression explained his destiny. In the trance state, he said that he was destined to suffer in this lifetime for what he had done in the previous one. It was a soul commitment that he had no intention of changing.

These two examples illustrate clearly why it is so important to be intuitive and love each child individually. There are no rules that will apply to all children. If there is one area in which we all need to be intuitive, it certainly is in our relationships with our children. Every child has a unique destiny, and if the parent is tuned in to the child's personality and uses intuition as a guide, incredible amounts of suffering can be reduced or avoided. Perhaps many individuals would achieve their goals here with considerably less stress.

While our relationships with our children are a most important example of why we should not try to coerce or control another person, but should accept people as they are, the same applies in all our relationships and judgments of others. For those of you who appreciate the great wisdom of the Christian Bible, consider the following verses:

Matthew 7:01 clearly states, "Judge not, that ye be not judged. For with the judgment you pronounce you will be judged" Three other passages I recommend reading are Deuteronomy 1:17, Romans 14:10-13, and Matthew 5:43-48. In Romans 12:19, we also find the statement, "Beloved, never avenge yourselves, but leave it to the wrath of God, for it is written, 'Vengeance is mine, I will repay, says the Lord.'" The twenty-first verse is one of my favorite quotes: "Do not be overcome by evil, but overcome evil with good."

Our social structure is replete with controversial beliefs and opinions that create violent conflict. One's skin color, ethnic background, sexual orientation, political philosophy, and religious beliefs all can create irreconcilable conflicts in all cultures today.

I believe the saddest controversy is over abortion. Some of those who proclaim the loudest that life is sacred do not hesitate to kill doctors and nurses. The truth is that you cannot kill a soul. When a fetus is aborted, the soul that would have lived in that body simply chooses another physical vehicle. The evidence for this is incontrovertible, in my opinion, which is based on my years of regression experience. In addition, souls choose their parents, so a baby is as responsible for its earth life as the mother or father and may have a variety of reasons for choosing such a body. If a soul needs the spiritual experience of being rejected because of some crime in a former life, for example it may select a mother who plans an abortion.

There is a famous clinic in Scottsdale, Arizona, where the doctor is conversant with this spiritual philosophy. This doctor reports many cases in which patients have sought help with unwanted pregnancies. The doctor, knowing that the soul is totally aware of the events concerning its development, explains to the unwanted baby that its mother cannot have it now for whatever reason. In a significant number of cases, there is a spontaneous miscarriage within days, and the mother is spared the stigma of an abortion.

Among my clients, I have had a number of young women who were suffering guilt from an abortion obtained earlier in their lives. Some were so bonded to their present child that they were certain that soul was the same spirit they had rejected earlier. In a number of cases, they were convinced this was the case when, in a trance, they saw an entire scenario explaining the reason for the timing of the child. In each case, the feeling for the current child was very special and brought the mother considerable joy.

One of my very close friends is highly intuitive and lives by her intuitive guidance most of the time. When her daughter was in college, she became pregnant and was devastated. She felt her life was ruined, and all her hopes for the professional life for which she was preparing were ended. Her mother said she communicated telepathically with the soul of the baby her daughter was carrying and explained that they were both sorry but the fetus would have to be aborted. She said that the soul laughed and said, "That's all right. I will come back later because she is to be my mother."

The young woman is now devoted to her career and does not want to marry. However, she wanted to be a mother, so she chose artificial insemination from a sperm bank for high-IQ males.

Her son is a genius. He has been on the cover of magazines and written up in numerous journals. He has a most unusual relationship with the grandmother who communicated with him before he was born. She has been his spiritual mentor, and their relationship is a joy to see,

Can the explanation of this young man's life be proven as I have related it? Certainly not, but the evidence is impressive, and it is consistent with other cases that have more impressive evidence. In addition, I have known this friend for many years, and her intuitive ability has been demonstrated to be accurate many times. Her integrity is recognized by all who know her.

I believe in the right of a woman to make her own decision. When one of my relatives became pregnant, she was very young and unmarried, and she asked for my advice. Her mother advised an abortion. Her friends were divided in their advice on whether to give her child up for adoption or have an abortion. When she called me, she was in tears and totally undecided. Her mind was spinning in confusion. I told her not to listen to others' advice but to her own inner feelings.

I pointed out that, if she gave up the baby, she would always wonder where it was. If she had an abortion, she would always feel guilty. If she kept the baby, she would be faced with many difficult problems. She must select which of three difficult paths she thought she could handle. She chose to have the baby, and her life has indeed been difficult, but she has never been sorry for her decision.

If we should not judge others or try to control their behavior, how can we maintain our own integrity and be faithful to what we believe while not interfering with the rights of others? Is tolerance relevant here?

Probably the basic attitude we must maintain is that we accept the right of any other point of view to be right for that individual or group. We do not try to change them by any kind of force. Often, however, we can change people by example. I have known a number of cases where one person in an office has changed an antagonistic group of people into a cooperative staff. An understanding of the power of our thoughts explains why this is possible. A positive attitude, one of concern for others, has power in a group.

I am reminded of one of my clients who reported constant verbal battles involving herself, her husband, and her two teen-aged sons. She hated the conflict but admitted that she lost control and screamed as loudly as the other three when there was a disagreement

She agreed to follow my suggestion, and the next time they all started yelling, she stopped and sat down at the table and said nothing. They all looked surprised and were silent long enough for her to say, "Why don't we all sit down and discuss this in a reasonable way?" She was delighted with the results and could not believe how it resolved the problems.

My husband and I were both very strong-minded individuals. We both had deep convictions about certain things. He had prejudices and habits that I abhorred. He listened to two radios and the TV at the same time so he could keep track of three sports teams. I hated that noise. We did not like the same music. We differed markedly about raising the children. He thought I was too permissive. I thought he was too harsh.

From experience, I know we can accept each other without conflict because he and I did it. When people ask the secret of our successful forty-nine year marriage, I have one answer: We never tried to change each other. Many times, I retreated to my study and reminded myself that he had just as much right to his opinion as I had to mine, so the problem was my attitude.

We all know people who truly get along with almost everyone. Take note of this. They are almost always popular. If they believe in some cause or project, they give their energy and attention to promote it. They correct something that may not be good by substituting something that is good.

Many years ago, a college student discovered a discrepancy in the student fund of a city college. In considerable righteous indignation, he took it to the school board. They were not about to accuse anyone or make a fuss, so they avoided any responsibility, even when he took them a copy of the ledger that clearly indicated figures had been changed.

In his determination to right what he considered a crime, he went to Sacramento and presented the case to the state board of education. They, too, were not about to meddle in a local situation, and after two trips to present his findings, he was beside himself with frustration. He was literally driven by the conviction that he had to right this wrong. He came to me for advice.

I suggested that, instead of using his time and efforts to punish the offenders, he turn his energy to helping people be honest and live with integrity. In other words, overcome evil with good.

In a few months, I heard from him. He had opened a print shop in Escondido and was writing metaphysical material and sending it out all over the country in the form of pamphlets and newsletters. I do not know how long he did this, but I had periodic samples of his work over a period of about fifteen years.

In spite of all the crime and evil in the world today, there are definite signs of hope for the future. I have ⸺ ᴵᴵᴵᵉ ᵒᶠ stories delineating groups of people who are really working to solve many of our social problems. Multiracial neighborhoods in many areas are cooperating in creating a safe environment for their children and providing help for anyone with special needs. The Riverside, California, *Press-Enterprise* recently published a feature story that was a heart-warming account of people caring for others, about a new organization called Teaching Tolerance that has spread rapidly through many schools.[1]

Efforts also are being made to reduce the violence among gangs. The *Press-Enterprise* reported two successful projects— one a drug abuse project, the other a solution for gang activity—that are producing positive results.[2] Successful job programs also are reducing the number of people on welfare and proving that most people want to work if they are given the opportunity.

Society can change only as individuals change. Everyone has influence with others, so your opinion does count. You can make a difference in the space you occupy.

Try to see the differing points of view of the people around you. If you really believe they are wrong, realize that quarreling about it will change nothing and will only increase the negativity. This makes enemies instead of friends.

I know it can be done because my friends and I do it. I have one friend with whom I disagree politically, but she does not know it. Why tell her I think she is wrong? It would solve nothing and damage a friendship of many years. Perhaps I can have more influence by remaining her friend and being a living example of my beliefs.

As you become more spiritually attuned, which automatically results when you begin to express love and compassion,

[1]"Love thy Neighbor," *Press-Enterprise.* Riverside, Calif.; January 14, 1999, p. Q1.
[2]"PeaceBuilders; *Press-Enterprise.* Riverside, Calif.; December 15, 1999, p. A-1, A-15.

you will find yourself guided by that inner voice that we call intuition. It becomes increasingly easier as you experience the results. The results are your own peace of mind and a sense of well-being within your world.

As your intuition kicks in more frequently, you will have the sense of being guided by a wise and benevolent force that keeps you on your own spiritual path. This does not mean there will be no problems, but you will have greater wisdom in handling those problems, and you will grow wiser for the experience. Best of all, you will begin to notice how things seem to work out for your highest and greatest good.

Synchronicity also will begin to manifest and be obvious to you. It will give you a new sense of security and a feeling that you are living in harmony with the destiny that is yours.

But please note: After working a lifetime to be accepting and nonjudgmental, I sometimes fail. Be patient with yourself.

10

≋

FORGIVENESS AND
ACCEPTANCE OF SELF

In the last chapter, we discussed accepting other people and
being nonjudgmental in our relationships as a way to increase
intuition and synchronicity. Many find this easier than accepting and forgiving themselves. Another word for this attitude
about the self is guilt. I believe guilt is such an important subject and so damaging to the individual that my last book, *Life
Without Guilt,* dealt with this subject in depth in an effort to
help people let go of guilt.

But a book on intuition also would not be complete without
the inclusion of a discussion of guilt because your intuitive
skills will be highly impaired if you do not believe you are
worthy of good things happening to you.

Examine your innermost feelings for a moment. Do you

think other people are better than you are, smarter than you are? Or perhaps you feel ugly or plain. Maybe you feel you have no talents and wonder why you are here. Possibly you are hiding some deep, dark secret, and you think if people knew about it, they would not like you.

I think it is no exaggeration to say that your happiness depends largely on your self-image. If your self-image is poor, it is like an insidious virus creeping through all of your thoughts and actions, literally robbing you of a healthy attitude about yourself.

The causes of this problem are legion. Many are the result of unfortunate incidences in childhood. However, if it is a deep-seated feeling of poor self-esteem, regression therapy is indicated and generally solves the problem. I believe the origin of many poor self-images is from a traumatic episode in a past life that then may be triggered or reinforced by a negative experience in childhood. It can almost always be alleviated by reliving that past-life event in an altered state of mind. The reason current psychotherapy is so ineffective in resolving this prevalent malady is because it has not yet recognized that the real source may be found only in some previous life.

A few years ago, I had a classic case of this kind of guilt. The young woman was married and the mother of two small children. When she came to my office, she was in mental turmoil. She declared that she was guilty of something horrible, but she did not know what it was. She was tormented with thoughts of burning in hell because her crime was so horrendous that it was not forgivable.

Her current history contained nothing that could account for her fears. She had loving parents and a happy childhood. Her marriage was a real love match, and she was completely happy as a mother.

She was readily able to accept reincarnation and willing to try a regression. This is not the usual procedure on a first counseling visit, but she seemed so ready that we proceeded with a trance. Within five minutes, she was in a deep altered state and experienced herself as a young girl of about fourteen, gathering herbs in a forest. She described what she was doing. She said her mother taught her about the herbs and told her she was doing God's work by healing people with them. Then the villagers brought a very sick baby and demanded that she heal the child. She knew it was dying and told the villagers she could not heal the baby. When the baby died, the villagers dragged her from her cottage, declared her a witch, and burned her at the stake.

I asked her why she felt guilty if she believed she was doing God's work. She explained that the priest in that life convinced her that she was an ignorant girl and that anyone who could heal was a handmaiden of the devil. He told her she would burn in hell forever because she could never be forgiven. She died believing this.

I asked her how she felt about it now. Who was right, her mother or that priest? She said, without hesitation, that the priest had been wrong. She was very relieved by this insight and expressed genuine joy as she came out of the trance state. A two-week follow-up on this case confirmed the success of her session with her all-knowing mind. She reported that the guilt feelings were totally gone.

Sex is something most of us experience, and it is frequently the cause of emotional problems. Since we are all sexual beings, this aspect of our lives is born with us and affects us from birth to death. I recall a young woman whose problem was triggered by an incident when she was still in diapers. She had enjoyed the pleasant sensation of rubbing her genitals. When her father caught her in this pleasurable activity, he spanked her and angrily ordered her never to do that again. She thought she was being punished for the pleasant feelings, and when she came to me for help as a teenager, she had unconsciously inhibited her development as a woman. Her breasts were not developing, and her menses were almost nonexistent. Her struggle to control her sensual feelings was the most difficult problem for her, since she had no control over those feelings and subconsciously believed they were bad.

Two regression sessions completely resolved the problem. Within six months, her breasts were normal size. Her menstrual periods began two weeks after the sessions and continued on a normal schedule.

Sex guilt also can have a powerful impact on self-image, even without apparent past-life involvement. I recall a visit from an elderly man dying of cancer. He was so weak I did not feel comfortable being alone with him and readily agreed when his wife wanted to come with him. However, I soon had the feeling that he was not at ease and could not talk freely in her presence. I suggested she leave the room and she willingly complied.

Though he proceeded to speak candidly, it was with considerable discomfort that he related an unbelievable story. He said that when he was seventeen, he had had sex with a classmate. That was the only time he had sex before he met his wife. However, he felt so much guilt over that experience that he had never been able to talk about it with his wife or anyone else. For a lifetime, he had lived with the terrible burden of having committed an unpardonable sin.

I found it difficult to believe that, with our current attitudes about sex, he could still hold that belief. However, when the incident occurred in his life, the attitude about sex was very rigid, and sex between an unmarried couple was considered a sin. He had been a sheltered young man raised in a Christian family and was totally unaware that sex was a common—if unspoken—activity. His marriage had been a happy one, and he still loved his wife, but for all of those years, he had felt as if he had been unfaithful to her.

All I did was give him some facts and figures about the normalcy of sex and assured him that he had no solid grounds on which to condemn himself so severely. The fact that I did not think he had committed a sin seemed to relieve him considerably.

He left my office looking much better and assured me that I had helped him let go of the guilt. When he died five days later, his wife called me and told me he had been at peace. She also informed me that she knew he was a deeply troubled man but she could never understand why. He shared the session in my office with her, and she was relieved and grateful to finally understand the man she loved. She said he had been a wonderful, kind, and thoughtful husband. In this case, his guilt may have made him a better husband. It seems sad that he had suffered so many years for so normal an indiscretion. Although there is no way now to know for certain, a past-life session also might have been valuable if he had not been so near death.

I grew up in a very sheltered Christian family and I realize now just how little I knew of the "ways of the world." When we moved and I attended a new high school, I was shocked and repelled by a girl in the shower room standing naked by her shower door who asked a fellow student to dry her back. I crossed her name off of my list of prospective new friends. She was not a "nice girl." In my senior year, I frequently did not understand the sex jokes the girls often told in some of my classes. I was married then, and they used to joke and suggest I ask my husband to explain them to me.

My first encounter with masturbation came from a friend of my husband. He brought this young man into our home, and we liked each other very much. It was much like a brother and sister relationship. One day, the friend told me that, if I knew something about him, I would no longer like or respect him. I assured him it would not make any difference, and he finally was able to get out the words that he practiced "self-pollution," the term often used for masturbation at that time.

I must admit I was a little shocked, but I did not let him know it. I told him that did not make him a bad person, and it would make no difference in our friendship. I realized from his suffering that this was something that needed to be better understood. I began reading what I could find about it. To my surprise, I discovered how normal it is.

As a matter of fact, any child who is not sexually responsive is not normal. I have a whole list of horror stories about parents who have punished their children for touching themselves in forbidden places. Is it any wonder that guilt from this normal activity is one of the most common forms of hidden guilt? If you suffer from this, do get yourself one of the many books written about it and find out how normal you are.

Guilt feelings, whether from present or past lives, also are common with other sex-related concerns, including incest, certain sexual practices, and fidelity. Incest occurs in all cultures and all times. In my practice, it was the unusual client who had had no incestual encounter sometime in childhood. Often, it was a mild experience. For example, I recall one woman who was still feeling guilty because she had sexual responses to the man next door who put his hands on her bare back under her clothing. She had been about twelve at the time. She said that she had felt "dirty" ever since.

When incest has been prolonged in the life of a child, it frequently causes permanent damage to the psyche. It also has been interesting to me that a close examination of many of the incidents reveals that the damage resulted more from the feelings of the victim, than from any physical harm. Often the client would explain that his/her pleasurable sexual response was the cause of the guilt. Since the sex act itself was supposed to be very sinful, it therefore must be just as sinful to enjoy it.

Extramarital affairs play a large role in the guilt arena, too, and yet are common. I have found that a majority of my clients had been in love with someone outside of their marriage at some time in their lives and for different periods of time, from weeks to years. I always explain that, when two people meet who have been together in a previous lifetime, there is always a soul recognition that is totally spontaneous and not within the power of the individual to control. However, what the two people *do* with the relationship is the important thing and determines the spiritual progress of each person involved. As with all experiences, there is a reason and a purpose in the encounter. Always the purpose is to promote the spiritual progress of the soul.

Sodomy and other sexual behavior considered not normal are not as uncommon as most people believe, but often carry heavy burdens of guilt and deep feelings of self-loathing.

Another area that snares many victims with guilt is the belief that you are responsible for someone else's misfortune or even for someone's death. Many cases in my files confirm this devastating guilt. Two illustrations will suffice to show the painful results and often foolishness, of this self-incriminating belief.

In the first case, the dynamics were very long and involved, but the point is that this woman was completely convinced that she had been the cause of her husband's death from cancer. She cried most of the time, and at the office where she worked, the staff was baffled because nothing they did seemed to comfort or help her. Since I knew her quite well, I finally suggested that she come to my office for a session.

She told me that her doctor recently had discovered cancer in her neck. It was in the early stages, and he wanted to start chemotherapy immediately. She was totally opposed to drug therapy as a treatment, and she asked me to help her get rid of the cancer.

This client had worked with me before. She was a very sensitive individual and an excellent trance subject. In an altered state, I asked her to see and know what the cancer was manifesting in her life. She immediately responded that it was expressing her guilt because she was responsible for her husband's death.

Following a very strong hunch, but not at all sure that what I proposed to do would work, I reminded her that since her husband had been gone only about a month, perhaps he was still near her. I suggested that she call him and ask him if he would come and talk with her. Almost immediately, she said he had responded and was with us. Her whole demeanor changed, and she reported to me that he was assuring her she had nothing to do with his leaving. In fact, he gave her three reasons why he had died, and they had nothing to do with her. He assured her of his love and begged her to forgive him for hurting her by his departure. He added that he was helping her to settle the estate of his parents, who had both died two weeks after his death and within days of each other.

She was so relieved by this revelation, which was totally real to her, that two weeks later the doctor found no evidence of cancer. In addition, she was no longer crying.

I must confess that sitting through a session that is so bizarre leaves me wondering just what really happened there. I can only speculate that spirits *can* communicate when conditions are right. I am sure of the positive results: Something apparently other-worldly is possible and brings about dramatic changes in people. Perhaps it all occurs in the subconscious of the individual, somehow guided by a higher wisdom in or *through* the individual. Was her husband's intelligent essence or spirit actually there in my office? Was it what some would call her imagination? We can only speculate at this point in time, but I have listened for thirty eight years to hundreds of cases of apparent interworld communications. I can testify to their reality for the client and the dramatic changes that occur in the life of the individual. More often than not, it brings about a resolution of the problem.

The second case I will share involving people who believe they have caused the death of another person is that of Marie, a young girl who was afraid to be hypnotized. She was in one of my workshop groups of high school girls who came once a week to my house to ask questions about metaphysics and parapsychology. They all wanted to experience hypnosis, so they had brought notes with their parents' permission. All of the girls were successful in being hypnotized except Marie. She was deeply distressed over this but totally unsuccessful, apparently because she feared being hypnotized.

Another girl in the group was a natural psychic, which I had previously recognized. Not wanting to exploit her gift, we did not use it in the group activity. The girls were fascinated by the paranormal field and mostly wanted to ask questions and discuss my answers.

On this particular day only two girls came, Marie and the one who was psychic. We waited a few minutes for the others because these two had seen them at lunch time and the others had said, "We'll see you later at Mrs. Denning's." Finally, I asked the two who were there what they would like to talk about. They immediately responded that they would like to "tip" a table.

We had discussed this phenomenon, but I had discouraged it. That day, however, it seemed right, so I brought out a TV tray, and the psychic girl sat on my left. I sat across from Marie.

I had never seen a table respond so rapidly. The moment our hands touched the table, it began to rock violently back and forth.

Marie looked across at me in wide-eyed amazement and said, "Mrs. Denning, my sister is here." The psychic said very calmly, "Of course, that is why we are here today. She wants me to tell you to stop feeling guilty about her death. It had nothing to do with you. You are *not* responsible."

The psychic then explained that Marie was afraid to be hypnotized because, in a trance, she might see that she really was the cause of her sister's death. This insight completely freed Marie of the guilt and the fear. At our next meeting, she achieved a hypnotic state with no difficulty.

The intriguing question here is, what prevented the other five girls from attending the meeting? If they had come, we would have spent the time discussing the topic that had been planned. There would have been no table tipping.

Although this is an excellent example of synchronicity, the question of intuition is a little more involved. Whose intuition brought this about? Perhaps Marie's spirit sister managed the entire scenario. Or possibly, the psychic, at a subconscious level, was responsible. It was she who suggested that we tip a table. The moment the table responded, she "knew" all the facts about Marie's involvement with her sister. She had not known before at a conscious level. As common as they are, at this point, we can only speculate on the modus operandi of the many strange events that occur in the field of paranormal experiences.

There are, of course, many other causes of guilt such as dishonesty in its myriad forms, from cheating on income taxes to stealing. The husband of a friend of mine committed suicide because he thought he had been dishonest on his income tax report. He was sure he would be in trouble with the IRS and perhaps be arrested. He could not face the disgrace. After his death, it all turned out to be a mistake, and he was not guilty of anything. His own moral code had been so rigid that he could not forgive himself.

The area of our subjective feelings and interpretations is also one that causes tremendous amounts of guilt and shame. My mother was a caring, loving, and unselfish individual, but she never could forgive herself for resenting her mother. I have counseled many clients who were unable to accept themselves because they could not forgive themselves for the resentments they carried toward some friend or relative.

One I recall well because she was not only a close friend but also a well-known minister in the community. In her second marriage, she was constantly harassed by her husband's first wife calling and making unreasonable demands.

She confided to me that she prayed constantly that her anger and resentment of the first wife be removed. She tried in every way she knew to love and accept her. She would feel as if she had succeeded, only to have her good intentions wiped out when the first wife called again. This struggle went on for a number of years, and she finally punished herself by developing cancer and dying.

When an individual is responsible for the care of an aging, and often invalid, parent, the desire to be free of this burden is a normal response to a difficult situation. In many cases of this kind, the caretaker becomes ill after the death of the invalid. The cause is frequently diagnosed as the result of the strain of the care given to the invalid. The truth might be that the caregiver is suffering from guilt over being glad the invalid is dead. This belief is a feeling few people can handle rationally. It is difficult to separate the wish to be free of the burden of care from a wish for the invalid to die. The former is a perfectly normal desire beyond our control, and the latter is interpreted as sinful.

I believe the time will come when we can accept death as a welcome relief from suffering and a happy transition to a new adventure. An East Indian guru once told me he could not understand our attitude about death. He said that, in India, they pray for the release of the soul when a person is nearing death. He was puzzled that, in the U.S.A., people do everything possible to keep others alive. He considered this cruel and selfish.

One last example of how a poor self-image is created is how the very methods of disciplining children in our society lay the groundwork for a poor self-image. It is important when raising children to differentiate between a bad child and a bad act. Since everyone makes mistakes, it is important to know the difference between the person and the deed. Children can be taught to learn from their mistakes, while at the same time maintaining their integrity as human beings.

Now that we have explored some of the causes of poor self-esteem, what can we do about it? First, let me say that praying for forgiveness will not solve your problem. Did it ever occur to you that God cannot forgive you until you forgive yourself? God has already forgiven you because he never condemned you in the first place. You have always been your own judge and jury. This fact has become very obvious to me through the many years I worked with past-life therapy.

In an altered state, communicating with the higher mind, clients always assume responsibility for the errors they have made and are able to forgive themselves for past mistakes. However, they often readily accept the problems they are facing as just and fair ways to learn the necessary soul lessons. It is interesting that this insight frequently reduces and, in most cases, eliminates the problems. God is not punitive and, therefore, the only purpose of pain is to teach us that something is amiss and we need to rectify it.

When Peter asked Jesus how many times he should forgive his offenders and suggested seven times, Jesus answered, "No, seventy times seven." (Matthew 18:21-22)

Let us look at the word *sin* for a moment. It literally means missing the mark, making a mistake. While Christianity teaches that sin is something bad, many other religions teach that you have to make mistakes in order to learn life's lessons. That is the plan of life on this planet. We are here to become loving personalities, and any digression from that purpose causes pain. The purpose of the pain is to alert us that we have made a mistake. It is not supposed to lock us into feelings of guilt and self-condemnation. Such responses actually defeat the purpose of the pain, for they concentrate our attention on the pain rather than on our spiritual progress. Remember, you are responsible for your own spiritual path and no one else's. Each person is accountable for self alone.

We all must find our true spiritual identity in our own way. Just remember, you are a divine expression of whatever God is. When you recognize that, you will learn to love yourself for your potential and then work to achieve that potential.

Many volumes could be written about the people who have successfully turned their lives around, working their way up from the lowest levels of degradation to become happy, productive individuals. This progress takes only determination and belief in yourself. When you accept your own divinity, your intuitive capacities will begin to manifest. You will actually be led to the kind of activities and actions that bring about major changes in your life. Love has the greatest power to change people. Jesus admonished us to love our neighbor as ourselves. Most people do not realize the profound implications of this. It implies that loving the self is of the greatest importance. Incidentally, all of the major religions teach love as man's highest goal.

Remember always that your mind is the creator of your destiny. If you choose to be a victim, you will always be a victim, attracting various forms of challenges into your life. If you have done something to harm another, spend your energy righting that wrong and then get on with your life. Changing your lifestyle, solving your problems, righting any thing you believe you have done wrong cannot be instantaneous. Life is a one-day-at-a-time adventure. Keeping your goal in mind leads you ultimately to that goal.

Above all don't get discouraged when you make mistakes. Accept your humanness, and let your mistakes be steppingstones to greater wisdom.

If you wish to develop your intuition, remember that loving and accepting yourself will markedly increase it.

11

≋

DEPENDABILITY

Do you know the true meaning of dependability? For one thing, it means being responsible. Did it ever occur to you how much havoc you can create by being undependable? A simple example of this is the person who is consistently late for appointments. You can adversely affect several people's lives by being late for an appointment.

I am thinking of a beauty shop that accommodates dozens of people a day. One late client can disrupt the schedules of not only the beautician but also of all the customers for the remainder of the day. As a result, some of them may miss important business appointments or be late picking up their children from school, for example.

Whenever you force other people to wait because you are

late, you have robbed them of their time. Few people ever think of themselves as thieves. However, we are when we force another individual to wait for us.

There are many reasons for being late, and of course some are legitimate. I am addressing the person who is consistently late to appointments. I have known many clients who declare they cannot overcome this problem even though they have tried. They plan ahead and try to start early for an appointment, but something always happens to delay them or prevent their prompt arrival.

There are many reasons for tardiness. Some people arrive late in order to be noticed by their peers, often making a grand entrance after everyone else is present. A few people enjoy making others wait because it gives them a sense of power. They enjoy the feeling of being more important than anyone else. The social butterfly wants to create the impression that she is so popular and has so many demands on her time that she can never quite keep up with it all.

This problem is another one that frequently can be resolved with regression therapy. The sessions for the problem are unique with each individual. One of my clients was a young man who could never manage to be on time. In a regressed state, he saw himself as a young boy about six. There was a circus in town, and he wanted very much to see it. His father sent him to the store and promised to take him to the circus if he was back in fifteen minutes. He ran as fast as he could to the store and back and made it within the deadline. When it was time to go to the circus, however, his father made some excuse and refused to take him. The child was so crushed and disappointed that he vowed he would never again put so much effort into meeting any deadline set by someone else.

That one session resolved the deadlock he had created within his own mind by his decision. He later reported to me that he no longer had any problem being on time for appointments. This is a perfect illustration of the power of our minds to create physical conditions.

He was a very sensitive young man and highly intuitive, having invented some significant pieces of machinery in his work in a munitions factory. His intuition was blocked in this one area of his life because of the vow he had made with himself in a moment of anger. Fortunately, such errors can be corrected when the individual is ready to face the spiritual law that has been violated. His resentment and anger at his father had perpetuated the problem, keeping it activated in his current behavior. When he realized the full import of his reactions, he could readily forgive his father as well as himself. With that insight, he was free of the symptoms.

Another important area of dependability is keeping promises. I have a friend who is a salesperson. I have seen her painfully inconvenienced many times by people who promised to call her or come to her office to complete a transaction, but they neither arrived nor did they call to cancel their appointment. This is an all-too-common practice and is the result of persons who cannot say "No" to a request. They would rather lie because it is easier. This is a reprehensible practice and the cause of much pain and suffering.

A similar infraction of ethical conduct is the person who accepts a responsibility such as being an officer in an organization and then resigns before the obligation is fulfilled. Admittedly, there are occasionally circumstances and unforeseen events which make this action necessary, but in the majority of cases, the excuse is a copout.

There is a saying, "His word is as good as his bond." The world would be a happier, better place if this could be said of everyone. I have been fortunate enough to know a few people like that. My husband was such a man. I saw him work when he was so ill his skin was pallid, because he did not want to throw extra work on the other people under his supervision. More than once, when he promised a businessman in financial trouble that he would help resolve a problem, my husband gave up part of his vacation rather than walk out and leave the man without financial advice through the crisis.

I recall how pleased I was one time when a businessman told me he had never met a man like my husband. He said they broke the mold when they made him. The man further stated that he had never in all of his business life encountered a man so caring and with such integrity.

My husband would never admit it, but he was highly intuitive and used his ability in his work at the bank. He could be counting a stack of bills and, if there was a counterfeit among them, his rapid counting would immediately stop, and he would remove that bill. With customers, he could almost unerringly spot the one who was dishonestly trying to pass a bad check.

While virtue may be its own reward, it is also true that virtue has other rewards. My life has been blessed with many wonderful friends. (I've had a few of the other kind, so I do know the difference.) I have worked with and enjoyed lasting relationships with many dependable people who are concerned about the welfare of others. Their lives have a quality that is far superior to the average person. They are happier in their chosen vocations, more successful in their business lives, and more compatible in their personal relationships. This does not by any means imply that they are spared the everyday problems of human beings. They have their share of flat tires, accidents, broken plumbing, deaths of loved ones, loss of jobs, and all of the rest of the problems human beings experience. The major difference is in their response to whatever problems they face.

The intuitive, dependable person just seems to know the right choices to make, the right responses to resolve dilemmas, and the best moves to create harmony in a variety of situations. They might well be called peacemakers, for they create harmony wherever they are. Perhaps their greatest reward is the love, support, and admiration they receive from the people who know and work with them.

The true meaning of dependability goes far beyond keeping appointments and living up to one's commitments. It is a quality of every personality that determines—in its presence or absence—the responses of each of us to the destiny we came to fulfill. In other words, every person must be dependable in carrying out his or her life's purpose. The person is fortunate who knows that purpose and allows no obstacle to stand in the way of its fulfillment. These people exemplify dependability in its highest form, and they are the architects who build the structures for all social changes and the advancement of humanity's understanding of self and the world.

They are found in every area of life, from the most sophisticated fields of science to the highest norms for human relationships. They are all well-known for their contributions, but we seldom think of them as destiny-driven people with highly developed intuitive skills. Only as we know the history of each one can we appreciate the sacrifices they have to make to achieve their goals.

They could certainly be called dependable intuitives, dedicated to helping human beings advance in their search for autonomy and spiritual maturity. One drive they have in common: to improve humankind's condition in this troubled world within the field of their own talents or skills. They seldom see themselves as special in any way. They are simply responding to a compulsion to act as they feel intuitively directed. Often, they admit that they believe God is the directing force.

Examples of these gifted people are legion. One of the most recent who comes to mind is the actor, Michael Landon. His life has been reviewed at length on television programs. Since I have followed his life for years, I have been delighted to see it given the attention it deserves. He was an excellent example in the entertainment field of a man with a mission. Against strong opposition from his colleagues in the film industry, he introduced *Little House On The Prairie* and *Highway To Heaven*. The public response vindicated his belief that programs with a spiritual message would be popular with viewers. His life expressed generosity, love, and service.

Edgar Cayce was undoubtedly the most gifted psychic in the twentieth century. It is true that he resisted his destiny because he thought it conflicted with his deeply religious beliefs. However, when he finally accepted that his gift was from God, he was instrumental in healing thousands of people and left information on the healing arts that is still used today.

Elizabeth Kenny (Sister Kenny), born in 1884, developed a successful treatment for poliomyelitis. She was so certain of the efficacy of this revolutionary treatment that she braved the persecution of the entire medical profession.

You may never have heard of Arthur Edward Stillwell, but from a poor childhood, he became a millionaire. He built the Kansas City Southern Railroad and the Port Arthur Ship Canal. He wrote thirty books. He credited all of his advice and direction for everything he built to voices who told him what to do.

In the field of psychology, there was Carl Jung, a man far ahead of his contemporaries. He was given only ridicule in universities as recently as twenty years ago, when I was working for my degrees in psychology. Now, his work is better understood and appreciated.

I have already mentioned Thomas Edison, George Washington Carver, and the Wright brothers, who contributed so much to our progress. And let us not forget Alexander Graham Bell, who gave us the telephone. All of these men claim their information came from a source outside of themselves.

I will share one story with you that illustrates in every aspect the idea of dependability in the use of intuition. Gail Ferguson was one of my early students, and we worked together for five years on a weekly basis. From the beginning, she knew that she had something important to give to the world and that there was some special way in which she was to use her psychic gift.

She is highly gifted intellectually and readily grasps concepts beyond the understanding of the average person. Her life was full of challenges, and she had her share of domestic problems, but she never wavered from following the intuitive directions that drove her life. For a number of years, she taught workshops to corporate executives in Europe and the United States. These workshops were an intense six-week course in how to use intuition to improve business.

She continued to use her psychic gifts to counsel the hundreds who came to her office, and later, after she closed her office, those who sought her help on the telephone.

A few years ago, she met a wonderful man who could appreciate a woman of her talents, and following their marriage, they set out on a voyage around the world in his yacht. For her, it provided the opportunity she had been seeking to finally write the book she had always dreamed of writing.

That book, *Cracking the Intuition Code.*, was published in April 1999. In a letter to me prior to its publication, she said, "This will be the climax of twenty-five years of dedicated research."

For Gail, believing in her intuition, being "dependable" in carrying out her life's purpose, has paid off for her, for those around her whose lives she has touched, and for all those who read her book and learn from her experiences. In the social structure of the current population, harmonious people such as Gail are like a new kind of society. The energy in such a group is very powerful. It makes one feel relaxed and accepted. Many times, attending meetings of people with this orientation, I have heard the remark, "I feel like this is my second family." In my own experience, I find myself in groups of many different interests and purposes all over the world—Russia, China, Brazil, England. But I always find this wonderful feeling of kinship wherever caring, intuitive, dependable people gather in groups for mutual, service-oriented activities.

I have been accused of being an idealist, and that is probably true. I can envision a world of people who are honest, unselfish, and caring about the welfare of others. I am personally acquainted with many people whose goal is to contribute to making a better world. I have had many clients whose primary concern when they came for counseling was to discover why they are here. They felt that they had some kind of a contribution to make to life, but they did not know what it was. Working toward increasing their intuition and using an altered state, they often were able to discover their purpose.

Never feel alone in your efforts to make a better world. Major changes come only when people lend their energy and activity in a joint effort to a specific purpose. Just remember, even though you do not know them, you have a lot of support from many others with the same purpose as yours. Look for the positive changes occurring every day around you and realize that your positive input is making a significant contribution.

In my file of inspirational sayings, I have the following. I do not know the source, but I will share it because I think it carries a powerful idea to use as a daily reminder of our responsibility to life:

> I am only one
> But I *am* one.
> I can't do everything,
> But I can do something.
> I will not let what I cannot do
> Prevent me from doing what I *can* do.

12

CREATIVITY

Do you think you have no creative ability? If you think that, you don't know yourself. Everyone has imagination, and that is all it takes to be creative.

One of my favorite stories is about a little boy who was in kindergarten. He was really concentrating on his drawing. His teacher asked him what he was drawing, and he replied, "I am drawing God." "You can't be drawing God," she responded, "because no one knows what God looks like." Without interrupting his work, the child responded confidently, "You'll know when I get finished."

Many years ago a father was watching his son play on the floor. It occurred to him that the child might enjoy a toy on which he could sit and move about. Thus, the original Kiddie

Kar was invented. There had been no small, three-wheeled toys before that for so young a child. All the neighbors who had small children wanted the new toy. The father was soon making them in his garage. He could not keep up with the orders, and the manufacturing of Kiddie Kars became a huge industry. They were simple, inexpensive, practically indestructible, and gave a small child amazing mobility indoors and out.

Sometimes one wonders where the ideas for new objects originate. It is certainly true that it must originate in some form someplace. Does the mind of the intuitive individual *pick* it up or *make* it up? In other words, does one create it out of nothing? Is there an invisible dimension that contains all of the energy blueprints of everything that has been invented or discovered? More important, is there an energy blueprint of everything that *will* be invented or discovered? Is there just one energy, since everything is said to be energy, and the mind creates new forms from that one energy?

Whatever the answer is, one thing is certain: We are all creating, all of the time, although the quality of our creations certainly differs. Some make a positive contribution to life, and others make a negative contribution. There are two classes of creativity. One is physical or material and includes all of the inventions on the material plane. The other is what we might call the realm of ideas. This is a vast territory and encompasses the social structure of all societies. Major examples in this second group include the Magna Carta and the Declaration of Independence. They both resulted from the creative ideas of people, and each idea was revolutionary at that time. Currently, we also have examples of this group in the multitude of global organizations created to improve the quality and life of people around the world.

Many people live daily lives of quiet frustration. They are the great majority. They may have low self-esteem, often feel unloved, may believe they are discriminated against, and often are sure they possess no talents of any value.

It is to this last group that I address some pertinent thoughts about creativity. Using the word creativity in the generic sense, everything we do is creative because our minds are always active, even when we are asleep. In the waking state, we are always creating our next move, our next activity.

Imagination is an important factor because it is what takes us beyond the ordinary mundane activities of our daily lives. The potential is in every individual to be creative on a higher level of productivity.

I had a friend a few years ago who was a high school counselor. She was deeply concerned about a group of students who refused to do their homework, frequently cut classes, and were behavior problems in the classroom. She was challenged to change the attitude of that group of underachievers.

She was a warm, caring person and knew how to bring out the best in students under her supervision. She decided to take over this class as their teacher and change their attitude and their performance.

I do not know just how she managed it, but she convinced them that they had the ability to express themselves in creative writing. They resisted her efforts at first, laughing at the idea that they could write anything worth reading. The eventual results were spectacular, however, and changed the lives of those students. Discovering they could create something worthwhile gave them a new perspective on their own self-worth.

This teacher read some of the essays to a group of us in one of her creative writing seminars. We were all amazed at the quality of the work those high school students had produced. The most exciting thing about the experience was, of course, the changed attitude the students had about themselves.

Another case is an even more dramatic example of how young people who are considered to have low intelligence or to be borderline delinquents can be changed. This friend came to me for help when her husband left her abruptly, with children and herself to support. She was an excellent trance subject, and in her first session, she had visions of herself working with children in a very special way. She was so convinced that she had been given a vision of her future work that she began preparing herself to be a teacher.

She was first a teacher's aide and so distinguished herself for two years that, when she applied for a grant to conduct a project, it was granted by the university. In her project, she set out to prove that she could raise the grades of the children in the elementary schools if she could have them for one hour a week. It was a very serious study and included control groups and supervision by a school psychologist.

The first year was so successful that she was granted a second year for additional study of her methods. She used relaxation and guided imagery with the children. In their relaxed state, lying on the floor with their eyes closed, she suggested positive images of self-esteem and well-being.

In the meantime, she had been working for her teaching credential and was eventually put on the staff of a middle school. She was given the seventh graders who were troublemakers and considered to be potential dropouts because they were unable to do academic work at that grade level.

She taught that grade for many years, and all of her students were especially selected for their inability to work successfully in a regular classroom. Her work was so remarkably successful that she was recognized all over the state of California, and many other teachers were sent to observe her methods.

When she faced a new class, she would put on a commanding demeanor and state emphatically, "I have a reputation that everyone in my class passes. Don't any one of you dare to spoil my reputation. I love you, and I am going to see that you all succeed." She did a lot of hugging and, at first, the boys were embarrassed by this and pulled away, but it was not long before they responded to her hugs and actually sought them.

What was the secret of her success? How could one person create such changes? In the first place, she was a warm, loving, caring person herself. She was deeply concerned about the many young students who experience failure at school. There was no doubt in her mind that her destiny was to help such students. The secret of her success, however, was in changing the self-image of those students. When they believed they could do it, they did. Their creativity channels were opened, and their performance reflected that.

This story illustrates the spectacular events that can occur when we follow our intuition. The early years of this teacher's struggle to achieve her education and raise her family were fraught with problems. However, her determination was bolstered by her continual contact with the vision of a new approach in the field of education. The details were not clear to her in the beginning, but she felt so secure in following her inner guidance that she followed that guidance a step at a time, knowing it would take her to the ultimate goal.

She is a perfect example of a person who came into this world with a special destiny of service and who responded by maximally using her creative ability, directed by her intuition, to accomplish that purpose. Hundreds of students are now productive adults because of her love and influence. Not everyone can accomplish what she did, but everyone does have the creative ability to be productive in some field. Your mind simply needs to be open to the idea that you are a creative being.

Another factor that must not be overlooked is motivation. Often, when the individual has a low evaluation of the self, there is little motivation to make any changes. This brings to mind another case history in my experience as a counselor. This boy was in the sixth grade and the object of his mother's deep concern. He seldom did his homework and did not want to go to school.

One day, he came home full of enthusiasm and wanted to know if his mother had a good book on science. It seems the school had hired an intern to teach science in the boy's grade. The intern was a young man and an enthusiastic teacher who, in the first class with the students, had inspired them to explore the subject. For the balance of that semester, he was engrossed in home experiments and constantly pouring over science books and articles.

When this teacher left, the boy organized a farewell party with gifts and speeches, and cried over the loss. He again settled into his old pattern of neglecting his studies. Unfortunately, in this case the creativity inspired by the teacher did not carry over, but it does illustrate the importance of challenging our children to activate their innate creative talents.

Another student of my acquaintance was in eighth grade and failing. One day, his teacher realized he was not seeing well. He was tested by an optometrist. His eyes could not focus properly from one line to the next, and so his reading often made no sense. As he left the optometrist's office following the diagnosis, he said to his mother, "Thank goodness I know why I can't read. I don't feel dumb and stupid anymore." He had treatments for his eyes and was fitted with corrective glasses. With his new attitude, he immediately improved in all of his classes.

Again, this illustrates the power of the individual's self-evaluation. As we become more aware of our human responses and attitudes, it is increasingly obvious how powerful our minds are in creating our experiences. The belief system we maintain about ourselves controls our creative capacities.

Knowing this is of paramount importance to parents, teachers, and all who work with and supervise children. What a transformed world we would have if all children were nurtured in an environment of love and encouraged to believe in themselves! We know that is an unrealizable dream at this point, but it certainly can be our goal when we realize the tremendous value to the human experience.

I have mentioned a few examples of *creating* physical things, but the field of improving products we already have is always wide open. For example, how about improving the ways we open food containers? Is there anyone who has not experienced frustration in attempting to open a milk carton? What about the plastic containers of nuts, cookies, pretzels, and numerous other edibles? One of the funniest short subjects I ever saw on television was a skit by Carol Burnett, trying to open the groceries she had brought home and ending up with all of them in the wastebasket. It made a delightfully humorous sequence but was, unfortunately, a true delineation of the condition of many of our product containers.

The fantastically sophisticated instruments used now in forensics to find and capture criminals are an incredible new field of science. They were all in the mind of someone before they were in physical form.

Modern surgery is another remarkable field for examples of the creative process. All of the instruments used now to transform bodies were unknown a few years ago.

We know the cotton gin, the sewing machine, the benzadrine ring, and many other discoveries or inventions were the result of a direct communication through the intuitive channel of their inventors. Two of the most prolific inventors who claimed their ideas came through the intuitive channel were George Washington Carver and Thomas Edison.

As for creativity in the idea department, examples are legion. Everything we experience daily is the product of someone's creative idea. Remember when you stood in separate lines at the bank and the post office? You looked at the lines and tried to pick out the shortest one. Finally, some one thought of a single line, which made waiting time equal for everyone. This is a simple example of how an idea can literally revolutionize the way we conduct business all over the world.

You, too, have such talents, though they may be hidden to you. Sit down, close your eyes, relax. Now tell yourself with conviction that you have untapped talents, that you are a creative, divine creation. Invite your intuition to go to work for you, and listen for any creative ideas that may come.

You may feel nothing that you can recognize, but know that

you have planted the request and know that your higher self always hears you. Often, the ideas or inspirations come hours or even days after you do this exercise. Of course, you have to believe in what you are doing. Just remember, you cannot fool yourself. Unless you mean what you say, it will not work.

Keep this thought in mind. The longer you hang onto your past, the less likely your future will improve. You can turn your life around—and increase your intuitive abilities—any moment you choose.

13

≋

LOVE

The ultimate goal of every individual on this planet is to learn to love. Few people understand or realize this. From all appearances, it would seem that the lesson has not been learned very well. It is a prominent theme in all religions. It is emphasized in certain types of psychology and education. All of the world's problems could be resolved by the application of the love principle. An analytical review of the power of love can leave no doubt of its efficacy in resolving conflicts between people.

To forgive and love someone who has harmed or cheated you in any way is very difficult and, for many people, impossible. But there is incontrovertible evidence of the power of love, and literature, religion, and my own case histories are full of examples of that power.

A subject so vital to an understanding of life on this planet cannot be adequately presented in one brief chapter, so I also have included a brief bibliography of selections that I have found especially helpful in understanding the importance of love in all of our relationships.

In 1955, M.F. Ashley Montagu's *The Direction of Human Development* was advertised as scientific confirmation of the enduring belief that human love is essential to all normal growth. Professor Montagu wrote from the standpoint of a psychologist. His vast research in biology and anthropology resulted in what he believed was scientific validation of the importance of love in all human affairs. He reported in detail some of the earliest studies of infants deprived of love and the results. Their accelerated death rate was sobering evidence of the importance of understanding the need infants have for physical and emotional nurturing.

Stella Terrill Mann's excellent exploration of love and its power, *Change Your Life through Love* came out in 1949. She stated that the purpose of her life was to help raise the consciousness of mankind. She also reminded readers that spiritual laws are above physical laws and pointed out that love promotes the welfare of persons and principles. In her final analysis, she said that she believed there can be no created good without love.

Dr. Erich Fromm was a truly great man who contributed much to the fields of psychiatry, psychology and psychoanalysis. He stated unequivocally that love is the only sane and satisfactory answer to the problems of human existence. *The Art of Loving* (1956) deals with the various types of love such as brotherly love, erotic love, self-love, love of God, etc. He believed that the social structure of western civilization is not conducive to the development of love and suggested changes that must occur if our civilization is to endure.

Eric Butterworth's *Life Is for Loving,* a hundred-page volume that contains an excellent treatment of love from numerous points of view, was released in 1973. I especially recommend his chapter on love and sex. He said in his final chapter, "Remember that love is the nature of the presence of God and of you in whom it is present, and that the great need in life is to be loved."[1]

One of the most famous psychotherapists of the twentieth century was Dr. Rollo May, author of many books in his field. His scholarly volume, *Love and Will,* is a masterpiece. He presented a detailed and insightful picture of the vast emptiness of our depersonalized technology, pointing out that this modern dilemma is the result of our failure to understand love and will.

Love Is Letting Go of Fear by Gerald Jampolsky, M.D., is a delightful departure from the usual. In the first place, his name is well known in connection with his work with handicapped children and with *The Course in Miracles.* This book is a series of excellent lessons about love, a story or a case history with each, and a closing affirmation for the reader, all accompanied by delightful illustrations.

One more excellent book is Leo Buscaglia's *Love.* Buscaglia's name has been almost a household word, since his writings and his many lectures in all parts of the country were very popular in the seventies and eighties.

In summarizing what it takes to be a true lover, he says you must have the subtlety of the very wise, the flexibility of the child, the sensitivity of the artist, the understanding of the philosopher, the acceptance of the saint, the tolerance of the dedicated, the knowledge of the scholar, and the fortitude of the certain. Since all of these are part of everyone's potential, they will grow and be realized as the person practices love. As love is expressed in each situation, our intuitive capacities increase because we are automatically tuned in to universal creative energy.

---

[1] *Life Is for Loving,* Eric Butterworth. Harper & Row, New York, N.Y., 1973, p. 97.

Another important source of information on the values and the importance of love are religious writings. I am talking about the Christian Bible, primarily, but also the teachings about love from other religions as well, since they all emphasize the importance of love.

In 1 Corinthians, I believe we have one of the most powerful expressions of love to be found anywhere. It has been said that a daily reading of this chapter will change a person's life, and I include it here in full, with the hope that it will inspire you to increase your efforts to love:

If I speak with the tongues of men and angels, but have not love, I am a noisy gong or a clanging cymbal.

And if I have prophetic powers, and understand all mysteries and all knowledge, and if I have all faith, so as to remove mountains, but have not love, I am nothing.

If I give away all I have, and if I deliver my body to be burned, but have not love, I gain nothing.

Love is patient and kind; love is not jealous or boastful; it is not arrogant or rude.

Love does not insist on its own way; it is not irritable or resentful;

it does not rejoice at wrong, but rejoices in the right.

Love bears all things, believes all things, hopes all things, endures all things.

Love never ends; as for prophecy, it will pass away; as for tongues, they will cease; as for knowledge, it will pass away.

For our knowledge is imperfect and our prophecy is imperfect,

but when the perfect comes, the imperfect will pass away.

When I was a child, I spoke like a child, I thought like a child, I reasoned like a child; when I became a man, I gave up my childish ways.

For now we see in a mirror dimly, but then face to face.

Now I know in part, then I shall understand fully, even as I have been fully understood.

So faith, hope, love abide, these three but the greatest of these is love.

Make love your aim, and earnestly desire the spiritual gifts.

Revised Standard Version of the Bible
1 Cor. 13 14:1.

The Bible contains many other passages about love. In biblical concordances, love has one of the longest columns of references. Here are a few that, kept in mind, can serve as daily reminders of the importance of expressing love in our daily lives:

Love your enemies and pray for those who persecute you.
Matt. 5:44

This is my commandment, that you love one another as I have loved you. Greater love has no man than this, that a man lays down his life for his friends.
John 15:12,13

Love one another with brotherly affection . . . Bless those who persecute you . . . Beloved, never avenge yourselves but leave it to the wrath of God . . . Do not be overcome by evil but overcome evil with good.
Rom. 12: 9-21

Love does no wrong to a neighbor; therefore love is the fulfilling of the law.
Rom. 13:10

Beloved, let us love one another, for love is of God, and he who loves is born of God and knows God. He who does not love does not know God; for God is Love.

1 John 4:8

Antedating Jesus was another great man who founded a religion and taught the same principles as Jesus. Here is a brief passage from the Buddha's writings:

> Our mind shall not waver. No evil speech will we utter; we will abide tender and compassionate, loving in heart, void of secret malice; and we will be ever suffusing such an one with the rays of our loving thought; and from him forthgoing we will be forever suffusing the whole world with thoughts of love far reaching, grown great, and beyond all measure, void of ill-will and bitterness.[2]

I believe few people know how far back in man's history the lofty ideals of love and concern for others have been promulgated. Many people think that they originated with Christianity. Nothing could be farther from the truth. I recall a discussion I once had with a minister of the Methodist Church. We were discussing the contributions made by various religions. I was extolling some of the writings in other belief systems, each one of which he tried to counter. Finally he said, "All right, but you will have to agree that Jesus's great contribution was that he taught us to love." Then I explained the Buddha's teachings about love, and he said, "Well, of course those teachings have been perverted." To which I responded, "Are you telling me that Jesus's teachings have not been perverted?" He had no answer for this because anyone who knows Christian history is aware of the many perversions suffered by Christianity as a world religion.

Most people have no idea how far back in time there were advanced souls who attempted to give human beings the rules

---

[2]"Faiths of Man," *Encyclopedia of Religions*, J.G.R. Furlong. Vol. 1, p. 366.

to live by in order to be happy. Krishna was born 3126 B.C., according to some historians. In the famous Bhagavad Gita, a magnificent treatise delivered by Krishna to Arjuna, the reader is given a picture of the larger arena of life, where ignorance and intolerance struggle against intelligence, understanding, and light.

Near the end of the poem we find the following:

> He shall have his feet directed on the shining path that leads to light, to happiness and love—going to the happy planes of those rewarded for good deeds and righteousness. For love is the crown of all our work, and love—the matchless crown of wisdom—God.[3]

It is interesting to note that all major religions have taught the golden rule. Taken in its true meaning, the golden rule implies loving one's fellow beings. The common paraphrase or Christian version of Matthew 7:12 is brief and straightforward:

> Do unto others as you would have them do unto you.[4]

Note that the equivalent major theme in all of the following is loving concern for others:

> Do not unto others what you would not they should do unto you. (Confucianism)

> Do not to others which if done to thee would cause thee pain. (Hinduism)
> In five ways should a clansman minister to his friends

---

[3]*The New Gita: An Interpretation of the Bhagavad Gita,* Wesley la Violette. DeVorss & Co., Los Angeles, Calif., 1955, p. 200.
[4]"So whatever you wish that men would do to you, do so to them," for this is the law and the prophets." (Matt. 7:12, RSV)

and familiars, by generosity, courtesy and benevolence, by treating them as he treats himself and by being as good as his word. (Buddhism)

What is hurtful to yourself, do not do to your fellow-man. (Hebrew)

No one of you is a believer until he loves for his brother what he loves for himself. (Mohammedanism)

As thou deemest thyself so deem others. Then shalt thou become a partner in heaven. (Sikhism)

Regard your gains as your own gain and regard your neighbor's loss as your own loss. (Taoism)

That nature only is good when it shall not do unto another whatever is not good for its own self. (Zoroaster)

In happiness and suffering, in joy and grief, we should regard all creatures as we regard our own self. (Jainism)

What I have shared with you here is the merest sampling of the vast literature we have on the power and value of love in human lives. You have to give it to get it. Perhaps that is where the greatest problem lies. The majority of people are seeking to find it from someone else.

For the person who has accepted the fact that all experiences are chosen by the self for the purpose of spiritual development and, often, for the completing of a karmic debt, there is no room for resentment or hate.

In the first place, hate sows the seeds of its own destruction. When you finally get the full implication of that universal law, you will think twice before you condemn yourself to whatever punishment your hate attracts. The behavior of your offender is totally irrelevant. It may deserve harsh punishment and, if it does, you may be sure it will come to that person. The important point here is that if you harbor hate, resentment, or anger, you have contaminated your own spiritual aura. By your act of aggression, you have given your enemy power over you.

I am talking about attitudes here. If the situation warrants it, such as in many crimes, there is a moral responsibility to report or testify against the offender, but not with hate or rage. Often, I have felt greater compassion for the perpetrator then for the victim because I was aware of the price that must be paid for hurting others.

Nurture compassion. It will help you see the pain and the cause behind many of the cruel acts of other people. An individual who has been brutalized as a child, either physically or emotionally, often does not have the capacity to act in any other way than with hostility. That is the stage they have reached in their own spiritual development.

If you think you cannot help your feelings, you are partially right. Love is not something you can turn on or off like a faucet. Learning to love is what life is all about because learning to love is the highest form of spiritual development. It can be done. I know a great many people who have done it.

I had a very good friend who was being chased one night, and she drove into an orange grove, trying to escape. She got stuck in the loose ground, and her pursuer caught up with her and raped her. It was a very frightening experience. She had two regression sessions with me, and I was amazed at the results. She concluded that, in her destiny path, she had chosen to have that experience. She recalled that, as a child, she had also been raped by an older cousin. In her case, it all apparently involved some unresolved karma with which she had to deal. I knew her well and saw her frequently. There was never any evidence of anger toward her attacker. She said she forgave him, and her behavior substantiated her statement.

One of the most powerful examples of the power of love I

have known occurred to another friend. She was a loving, compassionate lady who lived a life of service. One evening, an intruder forced his way into her house, and at gun point, ordered her to undress. She remained unhurried and perfectly calm as she was disrobing, all the time talking to him about himself, his feelings, and his behavior. When she finished undressing, she sat on the floor in a lotus position and continued to talk to him about himself. He was confused and totally unnerved by her behavior and responded to some of her questions angrily and defensively. Gradually, his demeanor changed, and he became more relaxed and less threatening. After almost an hour, he said in a bewildered tone, "Lady, I never met anyone like you before." He hastily left her house.

Some years ago, a young Japanese student was brutally murdered on the streets of New York. His friends from his Japanese village raised a sizable amount of money and sent it to New York to be used to help rehabilitate delinquent youth in that city.

During the Boxer Rebellion in China, two missionaries were killed in the slaughter. They had a son and a daughter who survived and were sent to the United Sates for their education. The purpose that drove them was to complete their schooling and return to China to teach love to the Chinese who had killed their parents. They accomplished their purpose.

What I am saying here is that it is possible to hate the deed and love the person. When your responses to life are coming from true love and compassion, your behavior will reflect that love in all of your encounters. Let's say you bump into someone on the street. Instead of saying, "Why don't you look where you are going?" you say, "I am so sorry. Please excuse me." Most people will respond by saying, "It was as much my fault as yours. I was not paying attention." Then you part with both of you feeling good about yourselves.

I have been verbally attacked many times in my life. When I was young, I responded quite normally and felt outraged. Then, in my early twenties, a painful experience taught me a beautiful lesson.

I was superintendent of a junior high department in my church. One Sunday, a young lady came to make an announcement, but she was too late for the announcement time and the group had already divided and were in their small classes with their teachers. She wanted to go into each separate group to make her announcement. I told her as kindly as I could that we never interrupted the sessions. I explained that, if she would come back at the end of the hour, she could make her announcement or I would make it for her. She was very angry and called me ugly names as she stormed off.

As I went to the window and watched her walk away, tears were streaming down my cheeks. I knew her and felt disappointed in her, for she was a beautiful young woman and generally very gracious. I actually felt how she would suffer from her behavior. I felt quite sure she would not know what to do about it.

I consulted the minister's wife, a close friend of mine, and asked her what I should do. She told me the young lady had also consulted her and expressed her chagrin and embarrassment. The minister's wife advised that she forget the whole thing and move on as if it had never happened. This advice pleased me because that was what I wanted to do. The next time we met at a church function, we both ignored the episode and, over the years, became lifelong friends.

Without exception, every time I have been verbally attacked, I have apologized for whatever I might have done that offended the other person. This requires some conversation, of course, and telling the other person you understand why they feel the way they do often completely disarms them and reverses their attitude.

There are no words to describe the wonderful feeling that permeates your entire being after encounters such as I have related. In such experiences, both individuals are winners, and no one is victimized.

If you enjoy a sense of power, this will do it for you. However, it is not a sense of power *over* others, but a special kind of power that cooperates with all of life's experiences and expresses as compassion and love.

It is true that horror stories seem to dominate the news. However, the vast majority of the population consists of honest citizens trying to be good neighbors and friends. If you are alert to them, there are many stories of heroism, sacrifice for others, and acts of compassion occurring daily in every corner of the globe. Look for the events that recount the many expressions of love and compassion that occur every day. You may be surprised at the number of people who put their own lives on the line for others. Booker T. Washington once said, "I shall allow no man to belittle my soul by making me hate him." This saying reminds me of a story about my great grandfather. One time when he had been mistreated, a friend asked him why he did not retaliate. His response was, "What? That would be lowering myself to his level. I cannot do that."

A March 1956 article in the *Christian Advocate* makes some highly relevant statements regarding hate and rage.[5] It quotes a New York doctor as stating that seventy percent of his patients had resentment in their case histories and that forgiveness would do them more good than pills.

I was particularly impressed by his comment on the vital organs of the body and their role in resentment. He stated that the vital organs of the body sit in constant judgment upon our moods. Our brain, heart, nerves, and blood pressure are the jury that condemns us when we harbor bitterness and resentments. He said, "Anger burns us up."

Since I am so firmly committed to the belief that man's highest achievement in this life is unconditional love and service,

---

[5]"How Love Cancels Hate," *Christian Advocate,* 1956.

this chapter is longer than most. Actually, I could go on for many more pages relating cases of people who love those who have hurt them. I believe, however, that I have given enough evidence of the benefits and importance of developing love as a way of life, that many of you will respond to the challenge and really work at it.

Do not be discouraged when you fail to meet your expectations. Above all, do not punish yourself for failures. I recall an episode in my life when I had a headache for three weeks. I finally called my favorite psychic friend and asked why my headache would not go away. She immediately picked up on it and told me I had lost my temper and given my son a tongue-lashing because his room was such a mess. Since I prided myself on never losing my temper with my children, I was punishing myself for this infraction. I reminded myself that I was human and that it was all right to make mistakes. Within minutes, my headache was gone.

This is an area where your intuition not only can benefit others but also can help you. Whatever question you may have about what is happening in your life, just sit down and relax, asking that you be given insight into the problem. When you can approach problems with love, you also will find your intuitive abilities increase.

I'll close this chapter with the first verse of "A Simple Prayer" by Saint Francis of Assisi:

> Lord, make me an instrument of thy peace.
> Where there is hatred, let me sow love,
> Where there is injury, pardon;
> Where there is doubt, faith;
> Where there is despair, hope;
> Where there is darkness, light;
> Where there is sadness, joy.

14

≋

THE UNIVERSAL FLOW

Intuition is the motivation that activates your responses to every situation you encounter in your everyday experiences. The more you respond to your intuition, the more you will be "going with the flow." Contrary to many who think that means maintaining a laissez faire attitude, it is just the opposite. It means a vibrant, active response to life's experiences. It requires acting *upon* events as they present themselves in your life.

It very specifically requires dealing with the moment, not crossing your bridges before you come to them. It was well expressed by Jesus when He was conversing with His disciples:

"Therefore do not be anxious about tomorrow, for to-

morrow will be anxious for itself. Let the day's own
trouble be sufficient for the day.

Matt. 6:34

The case of a young male client comes to mind here. He had
just graduated from high school when he came to me to help
him decide on a college. He had a driving compulsion to do
everything exactly right so he would follow his destiny path. At
that point in his life, he was questioning some of his decisions,
and he believed the selection of a college was crucial. He had
dreams of driving down the freeway and repeatedly being
steered to an off ramp and having to get back on the freeway. I
finally suggested he see a psychic. She told him not to be concerned about a college, that no matter which one he attended,
his destiny was a very straight road ahead, and he would end up
where he was supposed to be.

He was sure his destiny was to be a writer. He brought me a
sample of his writing in high school, and my silent opinion was
that he would never succeed as a writer. However, when he
graduated from college, he was recognized by the school paper
for an article featured in the graduation issue. It was very good.

Then catastrophe struck, and he was drafted into the army.
His mother was totally devastated. She tried a number of av-
enues to have his assignment changed to officer training or to
something else she felt befitted his talents or would keep him
from using a gun in combat. Her efforts were to no avail, and he
was assigned to a foreign station as a private in the army.

Then the great synchronicity of his life manifested, and he
was given a desk job as a reporter of activities on the base and
in the war zone. His entire time was spent writing articles and
reports to be sent back to the states for publication in various
periodicals and writing reports for military personnel.

When he was released from the army, he was immediately
successful in finding employment with a prestigious radio station, and in a very short time, he was hired as a writer by a

television studio. He has been an outstanding success in his field. *Worry is an exercise that guarantees failure.* Sometimes I wonder how long it is going to take for the human race to realize the power in that statement. Your mind is creating exactly what you do not want when you worry. Since the mind is a creative force, your worry thoughts are literally creating the experiences you fear. You are afraid of losing your job, so you give that idea power when you live in fear of it happening. You are afraid your spouse will abandon you, so you constantly think about that happening. Your fears automatically affect your behavior toward others, and your actions contribute to bringing about the very thing you fear.

The Bible has a simple but very profound statement to make about this. Isaiah 30:15 says "In quietness and confidence shall be your strength."

There are many references in the Bible regarding the handling of stress. Jesus said to the disciples, "Peace I leave with you . . . Let not your hearts be troubled, neither let them be afraid." (John 14:27)

Going with the flow does not imply passivity. Far from it. You are actively involved with every area of your life, wholeheartedly participating in each event and each challenge, responding to each experience by giving it your best reaction.

One young woman, for example, came to me for help after being divorced by her husband. He had fallen in love with a coworker. She still loved her husband very much, and they remained friends, She had given him his freedom without contest, believing that he could not help the attraction to this other woman. She attended one of my workshops for a number of weeks, and we became very good friends. She had a rare quality of love and always talked about her ex-husband with tenderness and understanding. When he and his new wife had a son, she loved that child and even babysat for them so they could go on vacations occasionally.

My own inner sense was that she and her former husband

belonged together, and I advised her to be patient and that some-day, somehow, they might be together again. I had met him and liked him. He was a really nice person and a very caring indi-vidual. A past-life regression revealed the reason she had to lose him for a period of time in this life. She decided to go back to school and, after earning a master's degree, she had found a very rewarding position.

Then I lost track of them both. A few years later, at a meeting where I was the speaker, they approached me after the lecture. They were holding hands and smiling, and I knew at once that they were together again. They had been remarried about six months. They looked like the proverbial newlyweds. I have sel-dom seen in two people the joy that radiated from their faces.

I had a chance later to talk with her, and she said that his second wife had divorced him, so he had been free to come back to her. This all occurred about four years ago, and I am glad to report that they are still happily married.

How did she go with the flow? She is a very beautiful person spiritually and loved so unselfishly that she could think of his happiness above her own. She believed in her own destiny enough to live each day in the best way she could, trusting that everything would work out for her highest good.

If you think such a response to life is easy, you are mistaken. She suffered tremendous pain during the years between their marriages. However, such pain accepted without resentment or rage builds a strong spiritual character. Believing that each event in your life is purposeful and has meaning helps you to go with the flow because you know every experience in your life has a cause and has a purpose. You may not know the cause or the purpose, but you can have faith in the system. Most people can understand the purpose only in retrospect. Then, it is often very clear.

I am going to share another case to point out the difference between going with the flow and pushing the stream. Sonia was a very close friend of mine and she, too, was divorced by her husband. She was a physically beautiful woman, with delicate features, eyes like limpid pools, and a soft, sultry voice that invited conversation.

About a year after her divorce, she came to see me and begged me to tell her why she could not find another husband. The desire to be married again totally consumed her attention. Because of her physical beauty, she had many suitors, but she told me that, after two or three dates, they never called again.

I told her to stop thinking of every date as a prospective husband and look upon the man as a friend and temporary companion. In three sessions, we spent a lot of time talking about living life each day for itself. She was a teacher, and I urged her to put her energy into being the best teacher she knew how to be. Above all, she was to believe that there was a life companion out there and they would be brought together when she was ready. I made it clear to her that she could not experience what she wanted by forcing it.

The universe responds to mental directives favorably only when we step aside and allow those forces to use their limitless resources to bring about the answer to our mental order. Keep in mind here that the universe has limitless resources with which to supply our needs, resources that we might not even think about. When we try to force things by introducing worry energy, it interferes with the harmonious, creative flow of energy that can be ours.

I told Sonia that every man she dated felt threatened by her intense desire for a husband. She promised to leave it to God, as she put it. Six months later, she called me to report that she was getting married to a wonderful man, and she was very happy.

That all happened about twenty-five years ago. The marriage has lasted well, and they have a teenage son who is a credit to them both.

I trust I am not confusing my readers here about having dreams and goals and plans for their future. It works in much the same way as making a blueprint of a building and then turning it over to the builders to make it a physical reality. When you use your intuition, whether you know it or not, you will have mental promptings to act certain ways and strong feelings about what you are to do. When you follow those inner promptings, you are literally living your destiny in a way that is for your highest good. It is then that the wonderful synchronistic experiences begin to be recognized as common occurrences in your everyday life.

At this point, you may be asking, "This all sounds good, but just how do I go about doing it? How can I be active and passive at the same time?" The answer is quite simple. It is all an attitude of mind. Actions follow your attitude automatically. When your attitude is a sincere desire for what is best for you and others involved in your life, the Universal Force responds to that.

The problem is that we do not always want what is best for us. Through my many years of counseling, I found most people have selfish agendas, and their actions, often dishonest, bring them only frustrations and unhappiness. No energy is more powerful than love and concern for the welfare of others. The application of love and concern can solve not only personal problems but societal problems as well. Let us hope that, as a society, we are moving in that direction.

My files are overflowing with success stories of people who, under the most severe adversities, overcame their handicaps and succeeded in making a useful and successful life for themselves. When their cases are analyzed, three attitudes become clear as driving forces in their lives: First, they believed in themselves; second, they believed that their goal could be achieved; and third, they believed that a force or power outside of themselves was cooperating with and assisting them. Some people call that force God. Others believe in guardian angels, mentors, or a higher part of their own souls available to assist them when they ask for help.

We each have a unique destiny. It is a mistake to try to emulate anyone else or to compare your purpose with the purpose of someone else. You may have a very short life here with a specific purpose. You may have a long life of service in some branch of science, education, the health field, etc. You are neither any more nor less important than anyone else. Perhaps you are to be the mother of a very important person. You may think your role is not important, but in the scheme of things, every person can make a significant contribution to society. It is very important to understand and accept your role and know that it is just right for you in your destiny or soul path.

I recall one young man who illustrated this principle. At eighteen, he was still trying to figure out why he was here and what his role was. He was a very serious young man with tremendous integrity and a deep desire to be of use in the world. One day he went to the theater, and a fire broke out. He carried eighteen people out of that burning building, and his own injuries brought about his death. As he lay dying, he was joyful, and his last words to his family were, "Now I know why I came, what my purpose in this life was."

As you can see, going with the flow as a path to intuition and synchronicity can take numerous forms, but its essence is the basic principle that gives new meaning to life as we are beginning to understand it in the light of the expanding consciousness of many people on the planet today. The following summary may provide a guide:

First—Desire, above all, to love and serve your fellow beings in some capacity.

Second—Desire what is best for you, even if it conflicts with some of your personal desires.

Third—Accept whatever occurs in your life as an opportunity for learning and spiritual growth.

Fourth—Use your intuition to look for the reason and purpose in undesirable experiences so you can change your attitude and correct those experiences.

Fifth—Be responsive to your intuition and rely on it as you experience its reliability.

Sixth—Recognize the synchronistic experiences in your life and appreciate and enjoy them.

Just how committed are you to improving your life? Wishful thinking will not do it. Nothing short of consistent application of these principles will give you the results you want. If you are genuinely loving and caring in your relationships, that attitude will enhance your intuitive ability and generate the power to act positively in handling the everyday problems of life.

This book is about intuition and using that wonderful capacity to follow your life path and to accomplish what you came here to achieve. The system is foolproof. To be successful, you must be in harmony with that system. I have given you a spiritual roadmap. Follow it and you will eliminate much of the stress in your life.

The goal for many of us is peace of mind, maximum use of our skills and talents, happy relationships with family and friends, and success in our vocation or profession.

All of these can be yours when you live in a state of constant harmony with yourself and the universe. No words can adequately describe the constant feelings of well-being when you *know* that you are in tune with and responsive to your own inner guidance. Problems become just passing events that you handle with the intuitive guidance constantly available to you.

Very simply put, the key—to intuition and to a fulfilled life—is attitude of mind. Sense the divinity within you and behave accordingly. Your intuition will flow, its guidance will be reliable, and, with complete confidence in the wisdom of the universal plan, you can relax and know that everything is working out purposefully and to the ultimate good for all, including you.

GLOSSARY

All-knowing mind—The higher-level or superconscious mind that gives humans, as more than physical organisms, everything about the self. It is this level of mind that is accessed in altered states such as hypnosis and that enables recall of past events, including past lives.

Clairvoyance—The ability to see people or events at a distance without using the physical eyes. Often used as another word for extrasensory perception or psychic ability. Clairvoyants are sensitive to energy fields beyond the known physical.

Ecumenical Council—Councils were held by the Catholic Church for the purpose of establishing and maintaining unity in the Church. Major decisions were made regarding theology and dogma. One such council in 1553 removed reincarnation from the tenets of the Church. At the same conference, the Apocrypha was taken out of the Bible because it contains references to reincarnation.

Entity—In a metaphysical context, the term applies to intelligent beings who no longer inhabit physical bodies. They are visible to a few people who are clairvoyant. They often are credited with providing help and comfort to individuals who pray for help.

Hypnotism—A method of preparing the conscious mind to relinquish conscious control. The subconscious mind is then responsive to the direction of the hypnotist. This is the tool most commonly used in past-life regression therapy.

Interworld communication—Communication with the spirits of people who were once living in physical bodies on the earth plane.

Karma—The universal law of cause and effect in operation. Fate, destiny, the current life experiences that are presumably the result of your behavior in the current life or past experiences.

Metaphysics—Beyond physics. A branch of philosophy that deals with first principles. An investigation into knowledge. A philosophical stance that all things are a part of one main source.

Paranormal—Refers to the field of parapsychology and metaphysics, which deals with any apparently nonphysical phenomena.

Past-life therapy—A technique gaining wide acceptance as a method of assisting individuals to recover memory of past-life experiences for the purpose of explaining and removing current fears, phobias, compulsive behavior, etc. Many physical symptoms can be relieved or removed using this technique. While it implies reincarnation, it is not necessary for the individual to believe in reincarnation to be helped.

Psychic—Any individual who is sensitive to phenomena beyond the five known senses. Psychics are aware of activity in the ethereal dimension. They frequently can see spirit forms and hear spirit voices. They may know events that are going to occur at some future time and may be able to intuit events that have already happened. Many people are born with this ability and, as children, confound their parents with information they have no ordinary way of knowing. It is important to know the difference between this normal gift and mental illness.

Reincarnation—An ancient and worldwide philosophical belief that all souls are infinite and on a spiritual journey to achieve perfection. The soul must experience many physical incarnations for the purpose of learning spiritual lessons and coming closer to the goal of spiritual perfection in each physical experience. Each experience is chosen by the soul for the spiritual lesson in it. Each problem is an opportunity to make soul progress if it is handled with positive energy. Reincarnation is completely compatible with Christianity and incorporates the major teachings of Jesus, such as unconditional love and service.

Spirit guide—Many people believe they have a spirit guide or guardian angel and that this celestial being accompanies them daily and assists them in various ways. For most people, this help is manifested in hunches or a subtle feeling that captures their attention. Others believe they are in constant contact with their spirit mentors. Volumes have been written providing physical evidence of the benefit experienced by people who have this contact with spiritual beings

BIBLIOGRAPHY

Bache, Christopher M., *Life Cycles: Reincarnation and the Web of Life*. Paragon House, St. Paul, Minn., 1994.

Besant, Annie; Leadbeater, C.W., *Thought Forms*. Theosophical Publishing House, Wheaton, Ill., 1925.

Beyer, Maximilian W., *The Purpose of Life*.

Blanton, Smiley, *Love or Perish*. Simon & Schuster, New York, N.Y. 1955.

Bowman, Carol, *Children's Past Lives: How Past Life Memories Affect Your Child*. Bantam Books, 1997.

Buscaglia, Leo Ph.D, *Love*. Fawcett Crest Books, 1972.

Butterworth, Eric, *Life Is for Loving*. Harper & Row, New York, N.Y., 1973.

Cerminara, Gina, *Insights for the Age of Aquarius: A Handbook for Religious Sanity*. Prentice Hall, Inc., 1973.

Daunter, Terri, *The Spiritual Dance of Life: When Two Worlds Meet*. Mobius Publishing, 1995.

Denning, Hazel M., *Life Without Guilt: Healing Through Past Life Regression*. Llewellyn World Wide, 1998.

Drummond, Henry, *The Greatest Thing in the World*. Dodge Publ. Co.,

Du Nouy, Lecomte. *Human Destiny*. Dodd Publ. Co. N.Y.,

Ferguson, Marilyn, *The Aquarian Conspiracy: Personal and Social Transformation in the 1980s*. J.P. Tarcher, Inc., Los Angeles, Calif. 1980.

Fromm, Eric, *The Art of Loving*. Simon & Schuster, New York, N.Y., 1956.

Gerber, Richard, *Vibrational Medicine: New Choices for Healing Ourselves*. Bear & Co., 1988.

Graham, David, *The Practical Side of Reincarnation*. Prentice Hall, 1976.

Hall. Manly, *Reincarnation, The Cycle of Necessity*. Philosophical Research Society, Los Angeles, Calif., 1967.

Harman, Willis; Howard Rheingold, *Higher Creativity: Liberating the Unconscious for Breakthrough Insights*. Jeremy P. Tarcher, Los Angeles, Calif., 1984.

Head, Joseph; S.L. Cranston, *Reincarnation in World Thought*. Julien Press, 1967.

Howe, Quincy, Jr., *Reincarnation for the Christian*. Westminster Press, Philadelphia, Penn., 1974.

Hunt, Valerie V., *Infinite Mind: Science of Human Vibrations of Consciousness*. Malibu Publishing Co., 1995.

Jampolski, Gerold, M.D., *Love Is Letting Go of Fear*. Celestial Arts, Millbrae, Calif., 1979.

Mann, Stella Terrill, *Change Your Life Through Love*. Dodd Mead, 1949.

May, Rollo, *Love and Will*. W.W. Norton & Co. New York, N.Y., 1969.

Montagu, M.F. Ashley, *Direction of Human Development*. Harper & Brothers, New York, N.Y., 1955.

Newton, Michael, *Journey of Souls: Case Studies of Life Between Lives*. Llewellyn World Wide, St. Paul, Minn., 1994.

Ponder, Catherine, *The Prospering Power of Love*. Unity Books, Unity Village, Mo., 1966.

Ponders, Margaret, *Laws of Love*. Unity Books, Unity Village, Mo., 1966.

Randall, Neville, *Life After Death*. Corgi Books, Transworld Publishers Ltd., London, England, 1975.

Rodegast, Pat; Judith Stanton, Ed., *Emmanuel's Book II: The Choice for Love*. Bantam Books, 1989.

Rogers, Carl, *On Becoming A Person: A Therapist's View of Psychotherapy*. Houghton Mifflin Co., Boston, Mass., 19xx

Sheldrake, Rupert, *A New Science of Life: The Hypothesis of Formative Causation*. J.P. Tarcher, Inc., Los Angeles, Calif., 1981.

Snow, Chet, *Mass Dreams Of The Future*. McGraw-Hill New York, N.Y., 19xx.

Sugrue, Thomas, *There Is a River: The Story of Edgar Cayce*. Dell Publishing Co., 1945.

Verny, Thomas, M.D.; John Kelly, *Secret Life of the Unborn Child*. Summit Books, N.Y., 1981.

Walker, E.D., *Reincarnation, A Study Of Forgotten Truth*. University Books, New Hyde Park, N.Y. 1965.

Walsch, Neale Donald, *Conversations With God: Book I*. Hampton Roads Publishing Co., Charlottesville, Va., 1995.

Whitton, Joel; Joe Fisher, *Life Between Life*. Doubleday & Co., Garden City, N.Y., 1968.

Woolger, Roger, *Other Lives, Other Selves*. Doubleday, New York, N.Y., 1987.

144

INDEX

A

AAUW 13
Abortion issue 35, 83, 84
Acceptance 27, 37, 46, 49, 75, 120
Adopted 81
Affirmation 58, 120
African tribes 18
Agapetus 16
Aggression 126
Airplane 53
Altered states of consciousness 59, 139
American Indians 18
Amethyst 55
Angel guides 5
Anger 32, 46, 69, 98, 104, 126, 129
anthropology 119
Antichristian 36
Antioch church 14
Apoplectic 46
Apparition 52
Appreciation 6
Architect 54, 60, 106
Architecture 72
Arjuna 124
Army 132
Arnobius 18
Artificial insemination 84
Artisan 54
Association for Past-Life Research and Therapies 22
Attitude 6, 25, 32, 33, 34, 35, 37, 43, 45, 57, 58, 69, 75, 76, 77, 85, 86, 89, 90, 112, 128, 131, 136, 137
Augustine, Saint 18
Aura 67, 68, 126
Auric field 46
Autonomous 31
Autonomy 41, 106

B

Basic principles 77
Behavior problems 43, 112

Bell, Alexander Graham 107
Benzadrine ring 116
Bhagavad Gita 124
Bible 6, 16, 25, 26, 82, 121, 122, 133, 139
Bigot 75
Blind spots 28, 32, 34, 35, 36, 38, 77
Blood letting 29
Blood pressure 46, 129
Blue Mosque 72
Blue prints 111
Bonaparte, Napoleon 20
Bowman, Carol 23, 24, 143
Boxer Rebellion 127
Bradley, Bill 63
Browning, Robert 20
Bruno, Giordano 19
Brutalized 126
Buck, Pearl 20
Buddha 123
Buddhism 125
Burbank, Luther 21
Buscaglia, Leo 120, 143
Butterworth, Eric 119, 143

C

Cancer 82, 92, 95, 96, 98
Cathedral 54
Catskills 71
Cause and effect 7, 26, 139
Cayce, Edgar 20, 22, 107
Cerminara, Gina 21, 143
Chance events 7
Charlemagne 20
Chemotherapy 95
Childhood 40, 77, 90, 94
Children 7, 23, 24, 30, 37, 40, 43, 56, 62, 63, 69, 78, 80, 81, 82, 87, 90, 94, 99, 102, 111, 112, 113, 115, 120, 130, 140
Christian 16, 17, 25, 27, 32, 82, 92, 93, 121, 123, 124, 129

Imagination 59, 60, 61, 62, 63, 65, 96, 110, 112
Immortal soul 77
Immutable laws 25
Impatience 39, 40, 46, 47
Incurable disease 56
India 17, 18, 99
Infantile paralysis 29
Infinite mind 51
Inner guidance 10, 114, 138
Inquisition 35
Inspiration 43, 109, 117
Integrity 41, 80, 84, 85, 86, 99, 105, 137
Intelligence 5, 6, 112, 124
Interworld communication 96, 139
Intolerance 124
Intueri 9
Intuition 1, 8, 9, 10, 12, 14, 30, 32, 37, 46, 49, 51, 58, 60, 62, 65, 69, 76, 81, 82, 88, 89, 97, 107, 109, 114, 116, 130, 131, 136, 137
Intuitive 34, 37, 49, 50, 53, 55, 56, 61, 67, 72, 81, 82, 84, 89, 100, 105, 106, 108, 111, 116, 120, 138
Inventions 51, 52, 53, 57, 61, 111, 116
Inventors 21, 116

J

Jacuzzi 63
Jainism 125
James, William 21
Jampolsky, Dr. Gerald 120
Japanese student 127
Jealousy 26, 69
Jerome, Saint 18
Johanites 18
Johnson, Raynor 21
Jot 25
Jung, Carl C. 21, 107
Justin, Saint 18
Justinian 16, 17

K

Kaballa 13
Kansas City Southern Railroad 107

Kant, Emmanuel 20
Karma 14, 15, 26, 27, 78, 126, 139
Karmic principle 77
Kelsey, Dr. Denys 21
Kenny, Elizabeth 29, 107
Kiddie Kar 110
Kipling, Rudyard 20
Krishna 124

L

Laissez faire 43, 131
Landon, Michael 106
Leibnetz, Gottfried Wilhelm 19
Life companion 135
Life decisions 30
Lincoln Monument 72
Lindberg 51
London, Jack 20
Longfellow 56
Love 23, 26, 27, 43, 45, 46, 80, 87, 90, 96, 98, 100, 101, 105, 106, 114, 115, 118, 119, 120, 121, 122, 123, 125, 126, 127, 129, 136, 137, 140
Lowell, James Russell 20

M

Maeterlinck, Maurice 20
Magna Carta 111
Major religions 17, 25, 101, 124
Mann, Stella Terrill 119, 144
Married 29, 43, 70, 90, 93, 134, 135
Mars 61
Masturbation 93
Mattel 57
Mattel Creations 52
May, William Rollo 120, 144
Mead, Margaret 21
Menses 91
Military parents 43
Milton, John 19
Mind age 61
Mind energy 36, 62
Mineral kingdom 55
Miracle 56
Miracles 52, 61, 120
Miscarriage 83
Modern surgery 116
Mohammedanism 125

Montagu, M.F. Ashley 26, 119, 144
Moon 61
Moral code 98
Moral responsibility 126
Mother 14, 21, 24, 29, 32, 41, 42,
    43, 44, 69, 79, 80, 81, 83, 84,
    90, 91, 98, 132, 137
Motivation 114, 131
Multiple birth theory 18, 23
Multiracial neighborhood 87
Music 40, 56, 86

N

Native American tribes 18
Nazarenes 18
Negative attributes 40
Negativity 87
Northern lights 71
Nurtured 115
Nurturing 119

O

Obligation 104
O'Neill, Eugene 20
Opal 55
Opinionated 32
Optometrist 115
Origin 16, 19
Orpheus 18
Oxford Movement 10

P

Pain 25, 27, 40, 46, 73, 76, 100,
    104, 124, 126, 134
Paracelsus 19
Paranormal 33, 36, 54, 97, 98, 140
Paranormal field 33, 36, 97
Parapsychology 36, 52, 96, 140
Passivity 133, 136
Past-life regression therapy 134, 139
Patience 39, 40, 42, 43, 44, 46, 47,
    48
Patton, George 21
Peace 48, 133
Peacemakers 105
Perfectionist 27, 47, 78
Perpetrator 126
Peter (disciple) 100

Philosophers 18, 19, 21, 120
Philosophical Research Society 18
Philosophy 17, 18, 20, 22, 23, 26,
    28, 37, 70, 83, 140
Phobias 23, 140
Piaget 10
Plato 18
Poe, Edgar Allen 20
Poet 56
Poliomyelitis 107
Popular 86, 106, 120
Port Arthur ship canal 107
Post Office 116
Power 1, 3, 5, 19, 26, 46, 58, 61, 64,
    65, 68, 69, 85, 101, 103, 108,
    115, 118, 119, 121, 125, 126,
    129, 133, 136, 138
Praise 43
Praying 99
Prejudice 30, 34, 85
Pressure 64
Previous life 23, 46, 59, 90, 94
Problems 25, 35, 37, 43, 57, 61, 70,
    76, 80, 87, 91, 112, 118
Progoff, Ira 21
Psyche 59, 94
Psychic 37, 45, 69, 97, 107, 132,
    139, 140
Psychoanalysis 119
Psychologists 20
Psychology 9, 64, 69, 107, 118, 119
Psychosomatic illness 31
Punishment 19, 42, 81, 100, 101,
    125
Punitive 27, 100
Pythagoras 18

Q

Queen Elizabeth 19
Quiet revolution 62

R

Rabbi Manassa ben Israel 17
Rage 5, 26, 35, 37, 46, 69, 126, 127,
    129, 134
Rainbow 71
Raped 126
Rapture 55
Rebirth theory 19

149

150

A.R.E. PRESS

The A.R.E. Press publishes quality books, videos, and audiotapes meant to improve the quality of our readers' lives—personally, professionally, and spiritually. We hope our products support your endeavors to realize your career potential, to enhance your relationships, to improve your health, and to encourage you to make the changes necessary to live a loving, joyful, and fulfilling life.

For more information or to receive a free catalog, call:

1-800-723-1112

Or write:

A.R.E. Press
215 67th Street
Virginia Beach, VA 23451-2061

DISCOVER HOW THE EDGAR CAYCE MATERIAL CAN HELP YOU!

The Association for Research and Enlightenment, Inc. (A.R.E.®), was founded in 1931 by Edgar Cayce. Its international headquarters are in Virginia Beach, Virginia, where thousands of visitors come year round. Many more are helped and inspired by A.R.E.'s local activities in their own hometowns or by contact via mail (and now the Internet!) with A.R.E. headquarters.

People from all walks of life, all around the world, have discovered meaningful and life-transforming insights in the A.R.E. programs and materials, which focus on such areas as personal spirituality, holistic health, dreams, family life, finding your best vocation, reincarnation, ESP, meditation, and soul growth in small-group settings. Call us today on our toll-free number:

1-800-333-4499

or

Explore our electronic visitors center on the
Internet: **http://www.edgarcayce.org.**

We'll be happy to tell you more about how the work of the A.R.E. can help you!

      A.R.E.
      215 67th Street
      Virginia Beach, VA 23451-2061